JAPANESE KANJI MNEMONICS JLPT N4

JAPANESE KANJI MNEMONICS JLPT N4

Lindsay Jimenez
Dioxelis Lopez

2022

ACKNOWLEDGEMENTS

First of all, I would like to thank my supporters of my first book. Without that type of support, I would have never finished writing this second book. The feedback, the messages, and the comments have been incredible. I would also like to thank those who have believed in me and my work. It has been a difficult journey, but I believe it has been worth it. I have learned the unimaginable and now my passion for Japanese and languages has grown immensely.

Now my biggest hope is that you enjoy this book as much as I did when I wrote it!

Book design by Lindsay Jimenez

Cover design by Harold Jimenez

English Edition by Pete Kuzmich

Formatting by Dioxelis Lopez

Copyright © 2019 JLPT Kanji Mnemonics JLPT N4

All rights reserved

No part of this book may be reproduced in any form without written permission from the publisher.

Contents

- HOW TO USE THIS BOOK 9
- ELEMENTS & RADICALS 11
- JLPT N5 KANJI 13
- STROKE ORDER RULES 14
- CHAPTER 1: TIME 17
  - 夕 EVENING 20
  - 夜 NIGHT 20
  - 早 EARLY 22
  - 朝 MORNING 22
  - 曜 WEEKDAY 24
  - 昼 NOON 24
  - 冬 WINTER 26
  - 夏 SUMMER 26
  - 春 SPRING 28
  - 秋 AUTUMN 28
- CHAPTER 2: NATURE 29
  - 林 GROOVE, FOREST 32
  - 森 FOREST 32
  - 薬 MEDICINE 34
  - 茶 TEA 34
  - 菜 VEGETABLE 36
  - 野 FIELD 36
  - 田 RICE FIELD 38
  - 海 SEA 38
  - 池 POND 40
  - 地 GROUND, EARTH 40
  - 飯 MEAL 42
  - 銀 SILVER 42
  - 風 WIND 44
  - 光 LIGHT 44
- 肉 MEAT 46
- 牛 COW 46
- 犬 DOG 48
- 鳥 BIRD 48
- CHAPTER 3: BODY PARTS 49
  - 心 HEART 52
  - 体 BODY, REALITY 52
  - 声 VOICE 54
  - 首 NECK 54
  - 頭 HEAD 56
  - 顔 FACE 56
- CHAPTER 4: OBJECTS 57
  - 物 OBJECT, THING 60
  - 事 MATTER, THING 60
  - 品 GOODS 62
  - 台 PEDESTAL 62
  - 図 MAP 64
  - 画 PICTURE 64
  - 服 CLOTHING 66
  - 紙 PAPER 66
- CHAPTER 5: PEOPLE 67
  - 私 I, ME 70
  - 自 ONESELF 70
  - 方 PERSON, DIRECTION 72
  - 族 FAMILY 72
  - 姉 ELDER SISTER 74
  - 妹 YOUNGER SISTER 74
  - 兄 ELDER BROTHER 76
  - 弟 YOUNGER BROTHER 76
  - 親 PARENT, RELATIVE 78
  - 主 CHIEF 78

員 EMPLOYEE, MEMBER 80

民 PEOPLE, NATION 80

医 DOCTOR, MEDICINE 82

者 SOMEONE, PERSON 82

CHAPTER 6: PLACES 83

場 PLACE 86

所 PLACE 86

屋 ROOF, HOUSE 88

室 ROOM, APARTMENT 88

家 HOUSE, FAMILY 90

門 GATE 90

院 INSTITUTION 92

館 BUILDING, MASION 92

工 CONSTRUCTION 94

堂 HALL 94

村 VILLAGE 96

町 TOWN 96

市 CITY 98

洋 OCEAN, WESTERN STYLE 98

区 DISTRICT 100

県 PREFECTURE 100

都 METROPOLIS, CAPITAL 102

京 CAPITAL 102

漢 CHINA 104

英 ENGLAND, ENGLISH 104

世 WORLD, SOCIETY 106

界 WORLD, BOUNDARY 106

CHAPTER 7: ADJECTIVES 107

明 BRIGHT 110

暗 DARKNESS, SHADE 110

青 BLUE 112

赤 RED 112

黒 BLACK 114

便 CONVENIENCE 114

重 HEAVY 116

軽 LIGHTLY 116

遠 DISTANT, FAR 118

近 NEAR 118

弱 WEAK 120

強 STRONG 120

正 CORRECT, JUSTICE 122

悪 BAD, WRONG, EVIL 122

短 SHORT, BREVITY 124

低 LOWER, HUMBLE 124

太 PLUMP, THICK 126

広 WIDE, SPACIOUS 126

寒 COLD 128

暑 HOT 128

CHAPTER 8: SPEECH 129

説 OPINION, EXPLANATION 132

試 TEST, ATTEMPT 132

文 SENTENCE, LITERATURE 134

字 CHARACTER, LETTER 134

問 QUESTION, PROBLEM 136

題 TOPIC, SUBJECT 136

不 NEGATIVE 138

以 BY MEANS OF, BECAUSE 138

理 LOGIC, REASON 140

度 DEGREES, OCCURRENCE 140

CHAPTER 9: ABSTRACT 141

音 SOUND, NOISE 144

意 IDEA, DESIRE 144

楽 MUSIC, CONFORT 146

業 BUSINESS, VOCATION 146

真 TRUE, REALITY 148

質 SUBSTANCE, QUALITY 148

力 POWER, STRENGTH 150

病 ILL, SICK 150

特 SPECIAL 152

験 VERIFICAION, TESTING 152

色 COLOR 154

味 FLAVOR, TASTE 154

料 FEE, MATERIALS 156

旅 TRIP, TRAVEL 156

元 BEGINNING, ORIGIN 158

同 SAME 158

CHAPTER 10: VERBS PART I 159

仕 ATTEND, SERVE 162

売 SELL 162

去 GONE, LEAVE 164

始 COMMENCE, BEGIN 164

回 TURN, REVOLVE 166

知 KNOW, WISDOM 166

死 DEATH, DIE 168

切 CUT, BE SHARP 168

代 SUBSTITUTE, CHANGE 170

貸 LEND 170

走 RUN 172

起 WAKE UP 172

用 USE, UTILIZE 174

通 TRAFFIC, COMMUTE 174

考 CONSIDER, THINK OVER 176

写 COPY, BE PHOTOGRAPHED 176

止 STOP, HALT 178

歩 WALK 178

住 DWELL, RESIDE 180

注 POUR, IRRIGATE 180

CHAPTER 11: VERBS PART II 181

開 OPEN, UNSEAL 184

研 POLISH 184

待 WAIT 186

持 HOLD, HAVE 186

急 HURRY, EMERGENCY 188

思 THINK 188

建 BUILD 190

帰 HOMECOMING, ARRIVE AT 190

作 MAKE, PRODUCTION 192

借 BORROW 192

動 MOVE, MOTION 194

働 WORK 194

進 ADVANCE, PROGRESS 196

集 GATHER 196

合 FIT, JOIN 198

答 SOLUTION, ANSWER 198

運 CARRY, TRANSPORT 200

転 TURN AROUND 200

勉 ENCOURAGE, STRIVE 202

別 SEPARATE, DIVERGE 202

CHAPTER 12: VERBS PART III 203

教 TEACH, DOCTRINE 206

好 FOND, LIKE 206

洗 WASH.. 208

発 DEPARTURE, PUBLISH 208

使 USE, ORDER, AMBASSADOR 210

映 REFLECT, PROJECTION 210

歌 SONG, SING.................................. 212

習 LEARN 212

着 ARRIVE, WEAR 214

有 POSSESS, EXIST 214

引 PULL.. 216

計 PLAN, MEASURE 216

究 RESEARCH, STUDY 218

産 PRODUCTS, GIVE BIRTH 218

乗 RIDE, BOARD................................ 220

送 SEND.. 220

終 END, FINISH 222

HOW TO USE THIS BOOK

The main goal of this book is to help those who are studying Japanese as a second language. For this reason, the book is centered on a specific Japanese Language Proficiency Test (JLPT) level. This second book of the Japanese Kanji Mnemonics Series focuses on the next 181 Japanese characters (kanji) found on the N4 level test. It assumes the reader has knowledge of the two Japanese alphabets (Hiragana and Katakana) as well as the 103 kanji required for the JLPT N5. In order to start using this book, please follow the following steps:

1. THE FRONT PAGE:
   a. Flashcard Style: The book is recommended to be used as flashcards. Therefore, the student will find the kanji mnemonic on the front page and the kanji information on the other side. Each front page contains a total of 2 kanji, which are related based on similarities such as radicals, same meanings, synonyms or antonyms.
   b. Mnemonic: The drawings have been made to match the characters' radicals, elements, and history as much as possible. In the cases where this was not possible, I just tried to make it easy to remember. However, creativity from the reader is also highly encouraged.

2. THE REVERSE PAGE:
   a. Common Meaning(s): The student will find the meanings that are most appropriate for the N4 level.
   b. Sentence: a sentence to help remember the kanji better and creates a story that can be used as a mnemonic device. Each sentence was formed by breaking down the kanji into different elements for easy memorization. The elements can be radicals, components, kanji or hanzi. Note: If you are confused about any of the elements used in the sentences, please refer to the "Table of Elements".
   c. Stroke Order: The order in which the kanji must be written.
   d. Writing Exercise: The student will have the opportunity to write the kanji in this section of the book for extra practice.
   e. ON and kun readings: These serve as a guide for the student to only focus on learning and practicing the readings that will be required in the exam. Note: When a particular reading does

not fall in either category, it will be noted as *Reading Exception*

  f. <u>Examples</u>: In this section of the book, you will find the following:
   - Vocabulary: The words chosen for each kanji in this book are words relevant to the JLPT N4. This is to give the student the opportunity to practice vocabulary found in the exam.
   - Furigana: All words contain their corresponding furigana on top of each kanji.
   - Abbreviations: In the examples you can also find the following abbreviations:
     - adj = Adjective
     - n = Noun
     - vi = Intransitive verb
     - vt = Transitive verb
  g. <u>Etymology</u>: In the case a kanji's history needs to be explained further, notes on etymology have been added.

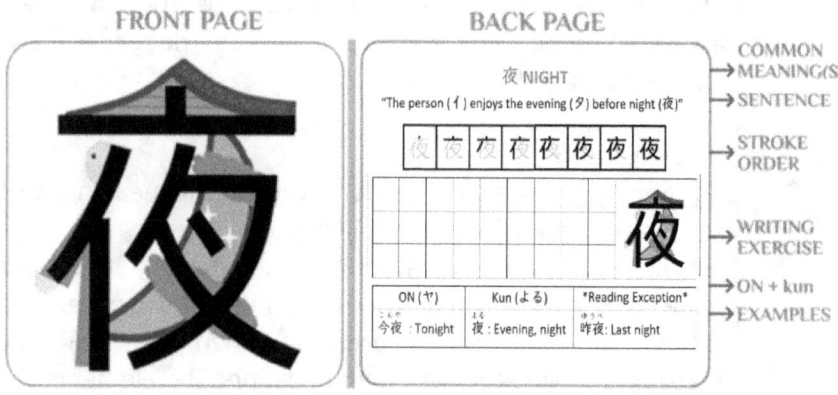

3. This book is not meant to be used on its own. It is highly recommended that the student also uses reading comprehension materials, such a fairy tales or books, as after seeing the different kanji in actual sentences it will reinforce what was learned in this book.

ELEMENTS & RADICALS

STROKE	ELEMENT	MEANING
1	亅	Hook
2	冫	Ice, two
2	又	Hand
2	ナ	Hand
2	亻	Person
2	厶	I, myself
2	十	Ten
2	儿	Legs
2	匚	Enclosure
2	力	Strength
2	𠂉	Bent person
2	冖	Cover
2	刀	Sword, knife
2	刂	Sword, knife
3	大	Big
3	寸	Measurement
3	艹	Plant, grass
3	辶	Road
3	ヨ	Hand
3	广	Tent
3	夂	Feet
3	氵	Water
3	土	Soil, ground
3	士	Man, samurai
3	小	Small
3	弋	Spike
3	己	Straighten up
3	女	Woman
3	弓	Bow
3	尸	Corpse
3	宀	Roof, house
3	子	Child
3	阝	Hill
3	阝	City
3	工	Work
3	巾	Cloth, scroll
3	口	Mouth, opening
3	囗	Enclosure
3	彳	Road
3	扌	Hands
3	也	To be
4	氏	Family, clan
4	方	Direction
4	文	Literature
4	斗	Dipper
4	歹	Death
4	开	Two poles
4	云	Cloud
4	攵	Hit, whip
4	欠	To lack
4	日	Day, sun
4	斤	Axe
4	耂	Old
4	灬	Fire
4	止	To stop
4	月	Moon
4	月	Flesh, body
4	尺	Measure
4	火	Fire
4	木	Tree
4	牛	Cow
4	心	Heart
5	穴	Cave, hole
5	目	Eye

5	禾	Grain		6	羽	Feather	
5	田	Rice field		6	⺮	Bamboo	
5	生	Life		6	艮	Good	
5	用	To use		7	里	Village	
5	王	King		7	言	Speech, word	
5	矢	Arrow		7	走	To run	
5	立	To stand		7	豆	Bean	
5	白	White		7	百	Head	
5	衣	Clothing		7	豕	Pig	
5	疒	Sickness		7	辛	Bitter	
5	石	Stone		7	貝	Shell, money	
6	冎	Bone		8	門	Gate	
6	㫃	Flag pole		8	尚	High status	
6	糸	Thread		8	食	Food	
6	虫	Insect		8	隹	Small bird	
6	羊	Sheep		9	食	Food	
6	米	Rice		9	頁	Head	
6	囟	Brain		9	昜	Sun rays	
6	聿	Brush		10	馬	Horse	

JLPT N5 KANJI

山	川	土	日	月	雨	水
木	天	火	本	魚	気	花
国	金	空	電	人	子	女
友	父	母	男	口	耳	目
足	手	社	車	店	校	道
駅	名	円	大	小	少	白
古	多	安	長	高	新	上
下	中	外	先	後	前	右
左	北	西	東	南	分	今
半	年	毎	何	時	週	間
午	一	二	三	四	五	六
七	八	九	十	百	千	万
入	出	生	立	会	行	休
見	言	来	学	食	買	飲
	語	聞	読	書	話	

STROKE ORDER RULES

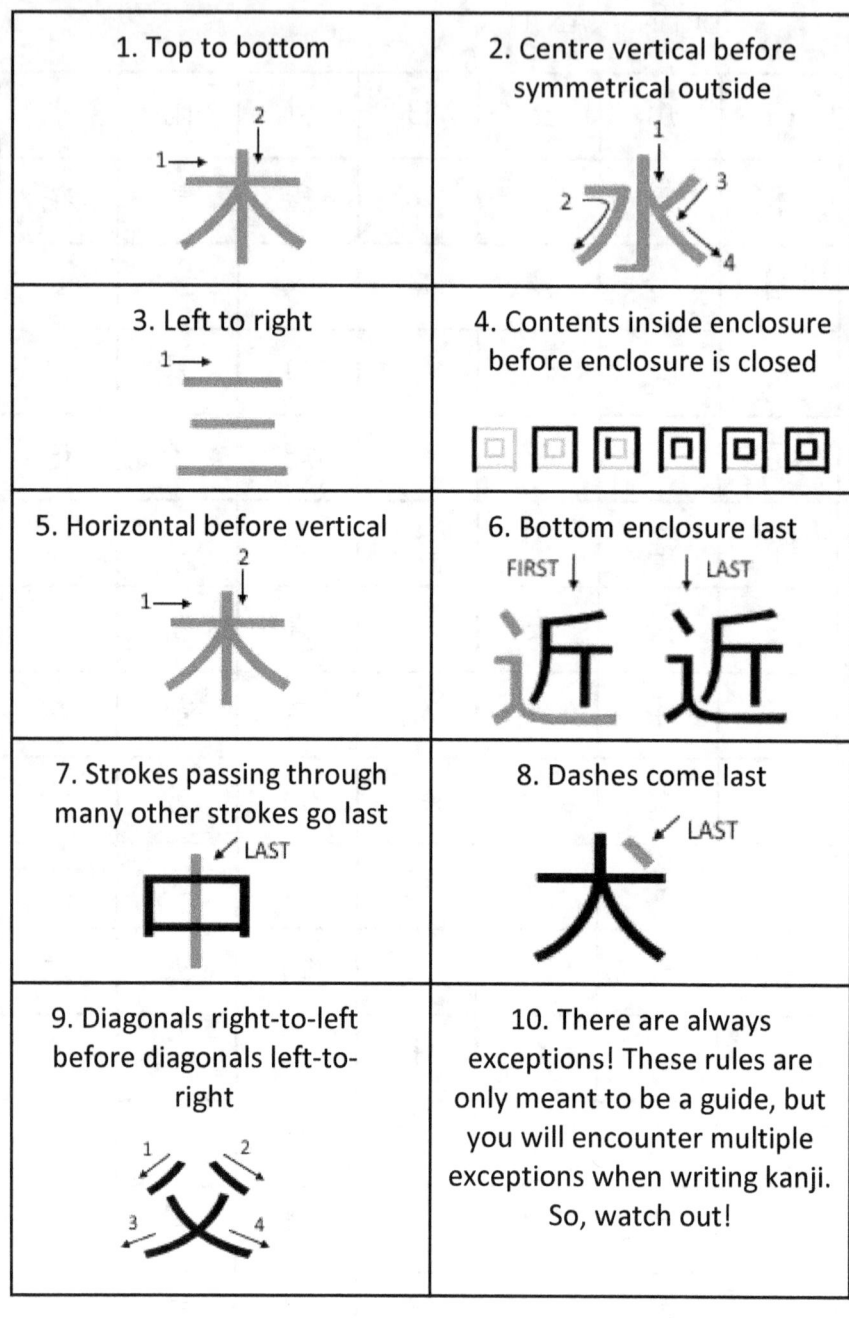

WHEN YOU LEARN KANJI:

1. Practice the stroke order

2. Practice the components/elements

3. Keep in mind the mnemonics

4. Read sentences that have the new kanji

CHAPTER 1: TIME

夕	夜	早	朝
1	2	3	4
曜	昼	冬	夏
5	6	7	8
春	秋		
9	10		

夕

夜

夕 EVENING

"This evening (夕) you can see the moon and the stars"

| 夕 | 夕 | 夕 |

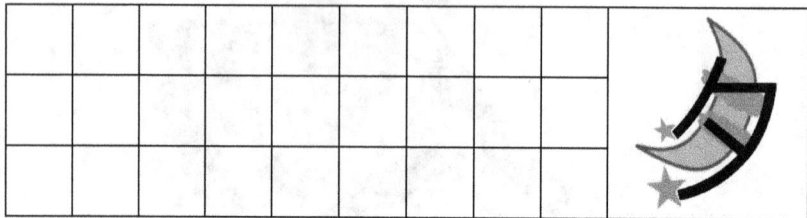

Kun (ゆう)
ゆうはん 夕飯 : Dinner
ゆうがた 夕方 : Evening

夜 NIGHT

"The person (亻) enjoys the evening (夕) before night (夜)"

| 夜 | 夜 | 夜 | 夜 | 夜 | 夜 | 夜 | 夜 |

ON (ヤ)	Kun (よる)	*Reading Exception*
こんや 今夜 : Tonight	よる 夜 : Evening, night	ゆうべ 昨夜: Last night

早

朝

早 EARLY

"I wake up as early (早) as 10 (十) in the morning to see the sun (日)"

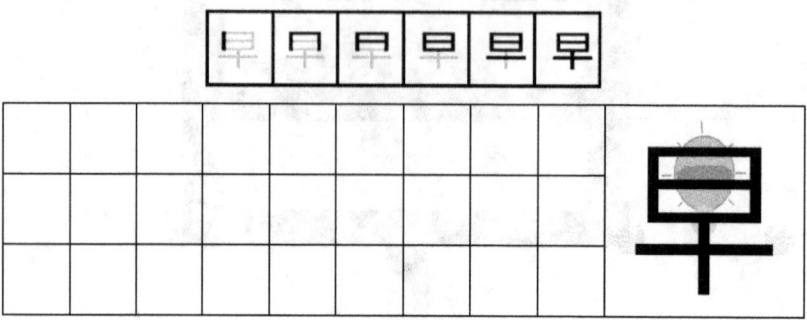

Kun (はや)
^{はや}早い : Early

*In the original shape of the kanji, it was the sun and a seed germinating.

朝 MORNING

"I can see the moon (月) very early (早) in the morning (朝)"

Kun (あさ)	*Reading Exception*
^{あさ}朝 : Morning	^{け さ}今朝 : This morning
^{あさ　はん}朝ご飯 : Breakfast	
^{まいあさ}毎朝 : Every morning	

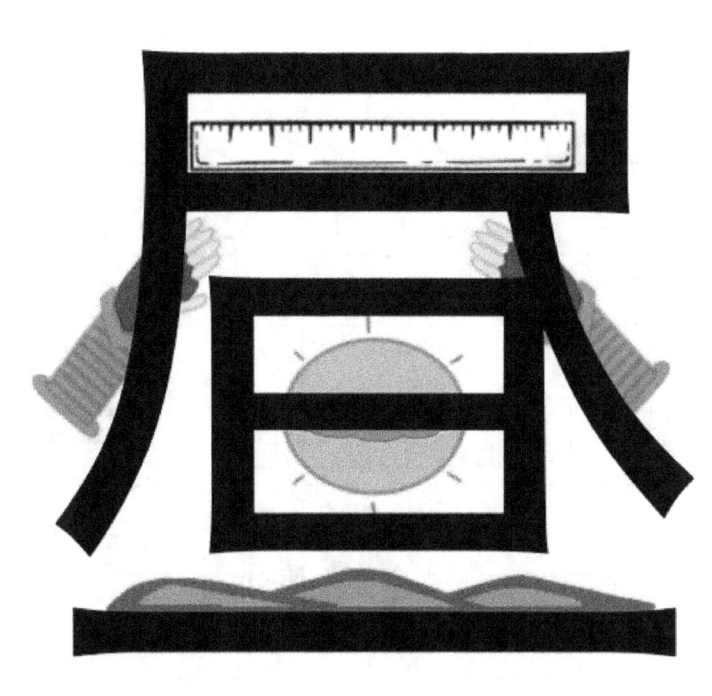

曜 WEEKDAY

"On weekdays (曜), I like watching small birds (隹) showing off their beautiful feathers (羽), while flying towards the sun (日)"

ON (ヨウ)

げつようび 月曜日: Monday	もくようび 木曜日: Thursday	どようび 土曜日: Saturday
かようび 火曜日: Tuesday	きんようび 金曜日: Friday	にちようび 日曜日: Sunday

昼 NOON

"Our ancestors used the sun (日) as a measure (尺) of when it was noon (昼)"

Kun (ひる)

ひるま 昼間: Daytime	ひる 昼: Noon
ひるやす 昼休み: Lunch break	ひる はん 昼ご飯: Midday meal

冬

夏

冬 WINTER

"There's a lot of ice (冫) and snowmen during winter (冬)"

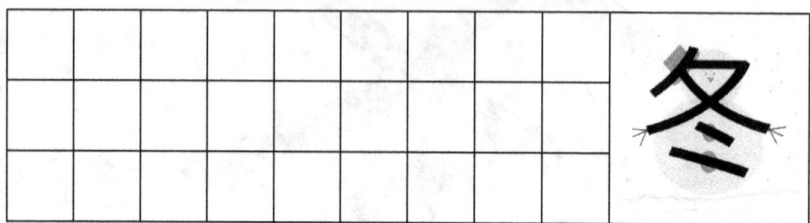

Kun (ふゆ)
冬 : Winter

*This kanji was originally a bent rope with a knot on both ends. This reflected the "end" of the four seasons.

夏 SUMMER

"The head (頁) master dances with his feet (夂) moving all over in the summer (夏) festival"

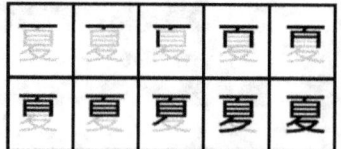

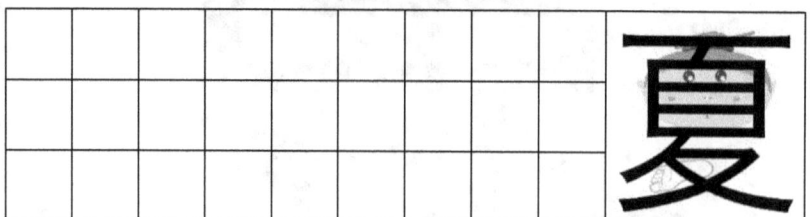

Kun (なつ)	
夏 : Summer	夏休み : Summer vacation

春 SPRING

"In the spring (春), the sun (日) is brighter and people (人) have flowers in their garden"

Kun (はる)
<ruby>春<rt>はる</rt></ruby> : Spring

秋 AUTUMN

"In autumn (秋), we clean the land with fire (火). Then we plant different grains (禾)"

Kun (あき)
<ruby>秋<rt>あき</rt></ruby> : Autumn

CHAPTER 2: NATURE

林	森	薬	茶	菜	野
11	12	13	14	15	16
田	海	池	地	飯	銀
17	18	19	20	21	22
風	光	肉	牛	犬	鳥
23	24	25	26	27	28

林 GROOVE, FOREST

"When you have at least two trees (木), you have a grove (林)"

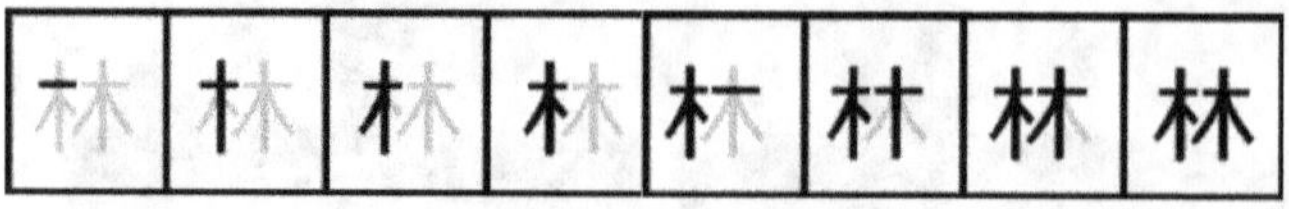

Kun (はやし)

林 : Woods, forest

森 FOREST

"Those are the biggest three trees (木) in this forest (森)"

Kun (もり)

森: Forest

薬 MEDICINE

"You must take your plant (艹) based medicine (薬) properly so that you can continue enjoying (楽) life"

Kun (くすり)

薬 : Medicine

茶 TEA

"I make tea (茶) with different types of plants (艹)"

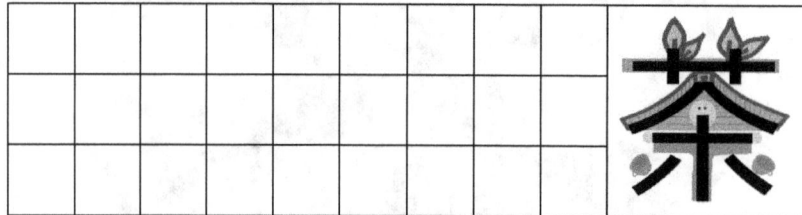

ON (チャ, サ)

お茶 (ちゃ) : Tea

茶色 (ちゃいろ) : Brown

喫茶店 (きっさてん) : Coffee lounge

紅茶 (こうちゃ) : Black tea

菜 VEGETABLE

"We gather (采) plants (艹) and vegetables (菜) for a living"

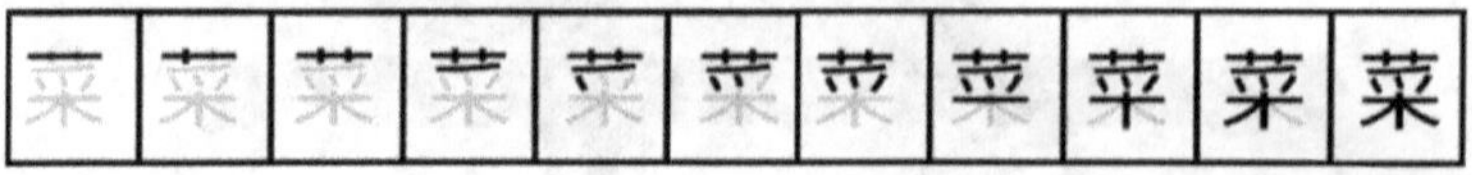

| 菜 | 菜 | 菜 | 菜 | 菜 | 菜 | 菜 | 菜 | 菜 | 菜 | 菜 |

ON (サイ)

野菜 (やさい): Vegetable

野 FIELD

"I will take care of the fields (野) in the village (里) myself (予)"

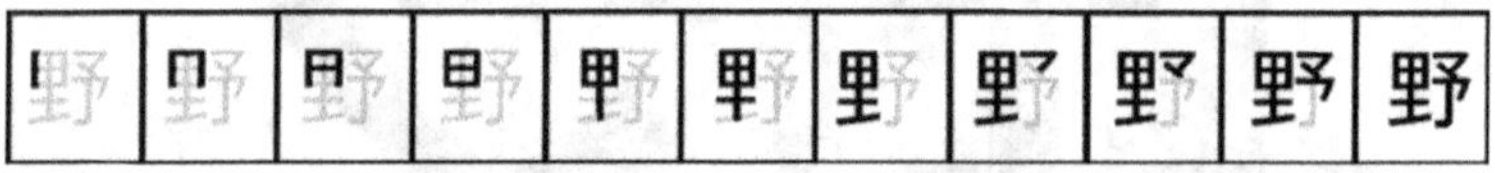

| 野 | 野 | 野 | 野 | 野 | 野 | 野 | 野 | 野 | 野 | 野 |

ON (ヤ)

野菜 (やさい): Vegetable

Kun (の)

野 (の): Field

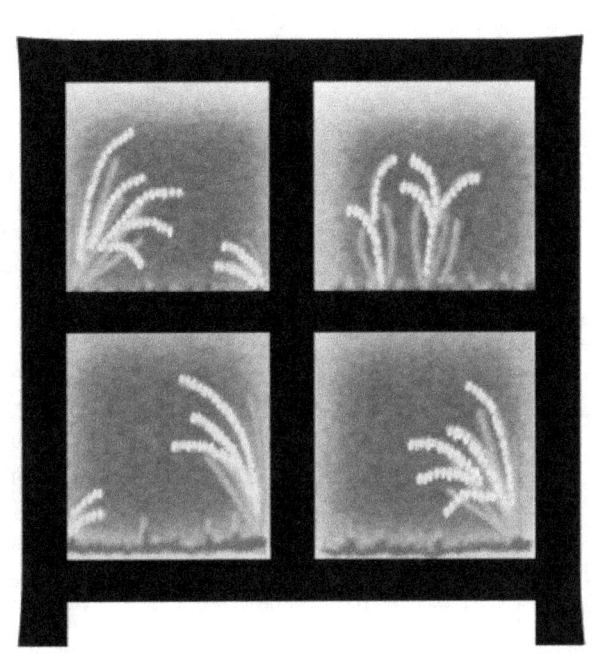

田 RICE FIELD

"A very nice, big rice field (田)"

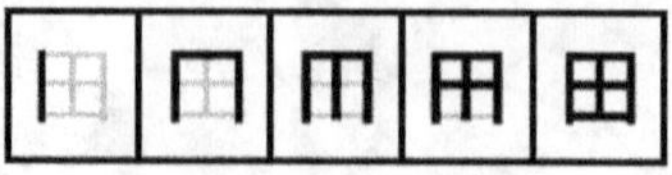

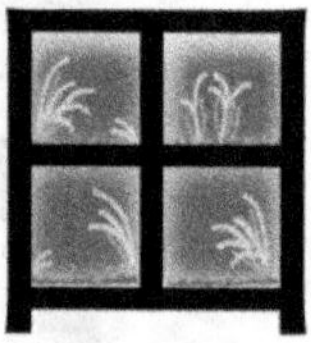

田 田 冊 田 田

Kun (た)	*Reading Exception*
た 田: Rice field	いなか 田舎: Countryside

海 SEA

"Every (毎) drop of water (氵) goes back to the sea (海)"

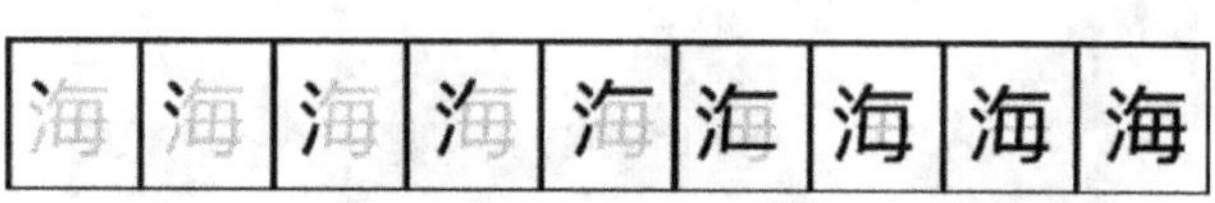

海 海 海 海 海 海 海 海 海

ON (カイ)	Kun (うみ)
かいがん 海岸: Coast	うみ 海: Sea

池 POND

"The water (氵) in this pond (池) is (也) drying out"

Kun (いけ)
^{いけ}池: Pond

地 GROUND, EARTH

"And this is (也) the ground (地) with plants and soil (土) all over"

ON (チ, ジ)	
^{ちかてつ}地下鉄: Underground train	^{ちり}地理: Geography
^{じしん}地震: Earthquake	^{ちず}地図: Map

飯 MEAL

"Don't be against (反) the party. Instead eat tons of food (食) during the meal (飯)"

ON (ハン)

朝ご飯 (あさごはん): Breakfast
晩ご飯 (ばんごはん): Dinner
夕飯 (ゆうはん): Dinner
ご飯 (ごはん): Cooked rice
昼ご飯 (ひるごはん): Lunch

銀 SILVER

"Silver (銀) can be as good (艮) as gold (金)"

ON (ギン)

銀行 (ぎんこう): Bank

風 WIND

"Even during strong winds (風), the insect (虫) keeps on flying"

ON (フウ, フ)	Kun (かぜ, か)
たいふう 台風: Typhoon	かぜ 風: Wind
ふろ お風呂: Bath	かぜ 風邪: Cold (illness)

*Originally it was a bird (not an insect) and it was considered the god of wind.

光 LIGHT

"The table with wooden legs (儿) is holding the light (光) that sparkles like fire (火)"

Kun (ひか, ひかり)
ひか 光る: To shine, to glitter
ひかり 光: Light

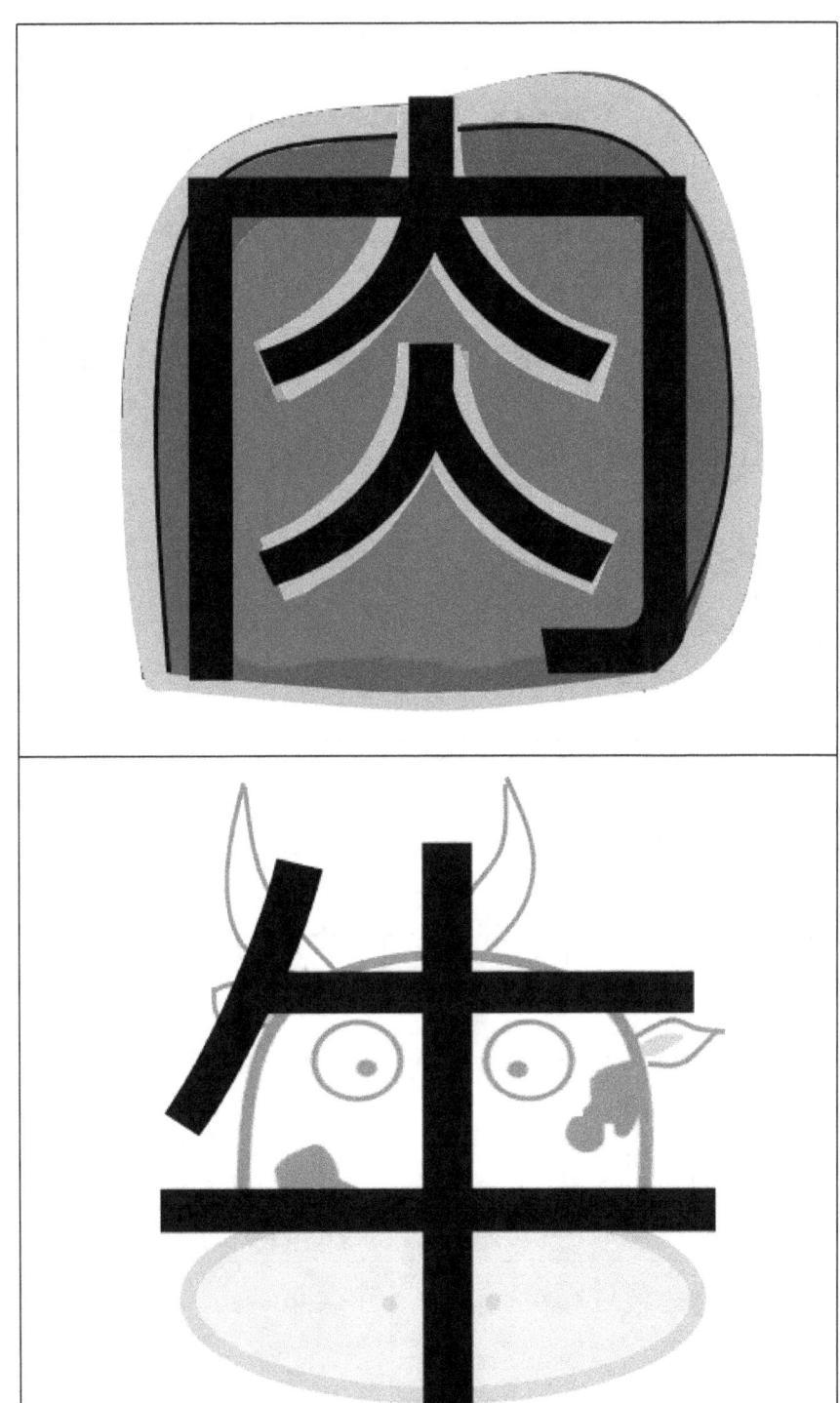

肉 MEAT

"The meat (肉) is a bit burned"

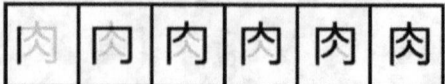

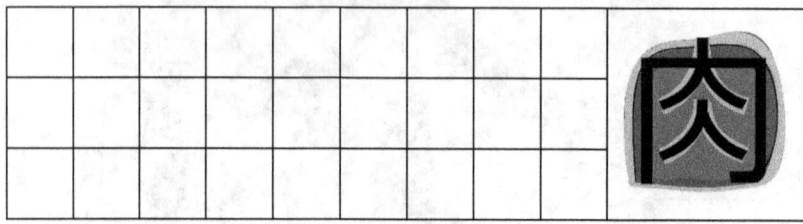

ON (ニク)

<ruby>肉<rt>にく</rt></ruby> : Meat

とり<ruby>肉<rt>にく</rt></ruby> : Chicken meat

<ruby>牛肉<rt>ぎゅうにく</rt></ruby> : Beef

<ruby>豚肉<rt>ぶたにく</rt></ruby> : Pork

牛 COW

"Look at the cow's (牛) head and its two horns"

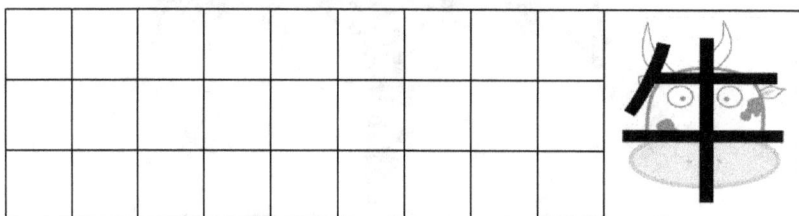

ON (ギュウ)

<ruby>牛肉<rt>ぎゅうにく</rt></ruby> : Beef

<ruby>牛乳<rt>ぎゅうにゅう</rt></ruby> : Milk

Kun (うし)

<ruby>牛<rt>うし</rt></ruby> : Cattle, cow

犬 DOG

"A dog (犬) with a big (大) bone and a long tail"

| 大 | 大 | 犬 | 犬 |

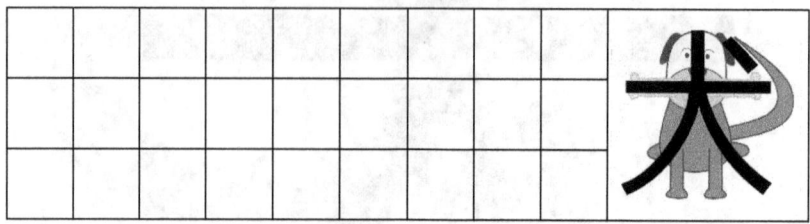

Kun (いぬ)
^{いぬ}犬: Dog

鳥 BIRD

"Some birds (鳥) have a crest"

| 鳥 | 鳥 | 鳥 | 鳥 | 鳥 | 鳥 | 鳥 | 鳥 | 鳥 | 鳥 | 鳥 |

Kun (とり)
^{とり}鳥: Bird
^{ことり}小鳥: Small bird

CHAPTER 3: BODY PARTS

心	体	声	首	頭	顔
29	30	31	32	33	34

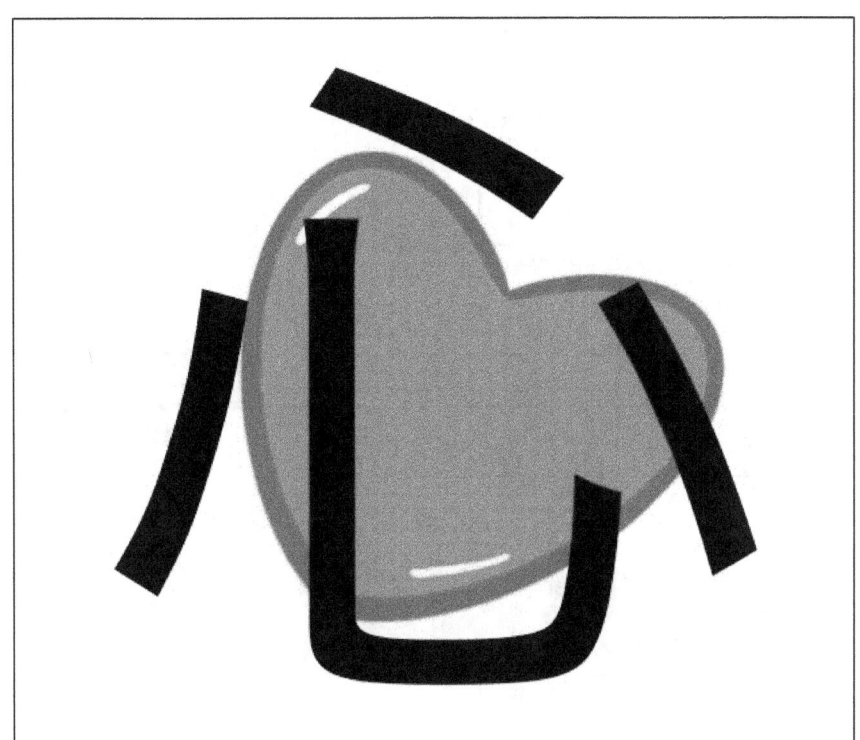

心 HEART

"The heart (心) in this drawing is tilted to the right"

ON (シン)	Kun (こころ)
<ruby>安心<rt>あんしん</rt></ruby>：Relief <ruby>心配<rt>しんぱい</rt></ruby>: Worry	<ruby>心<rt>こころ</rt></ruby>：Heart

体 BODY, REALITY

"A person's (亻) body (体) isn't just made out of flesh, but also from the knowledge gained through reading books (本)"

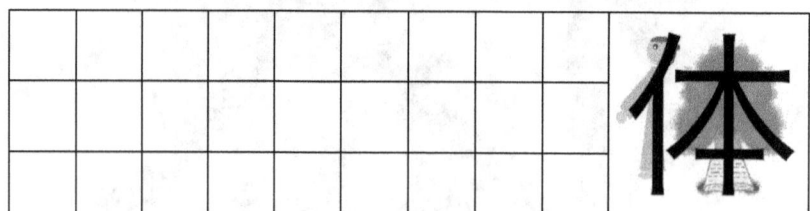

ON (タイ)	Kun (からだ)
<ruby>大体<rt>だいたい</rt></ruby>：Generally	<ruby>体<rt>からだ</rt></ruby>：Body

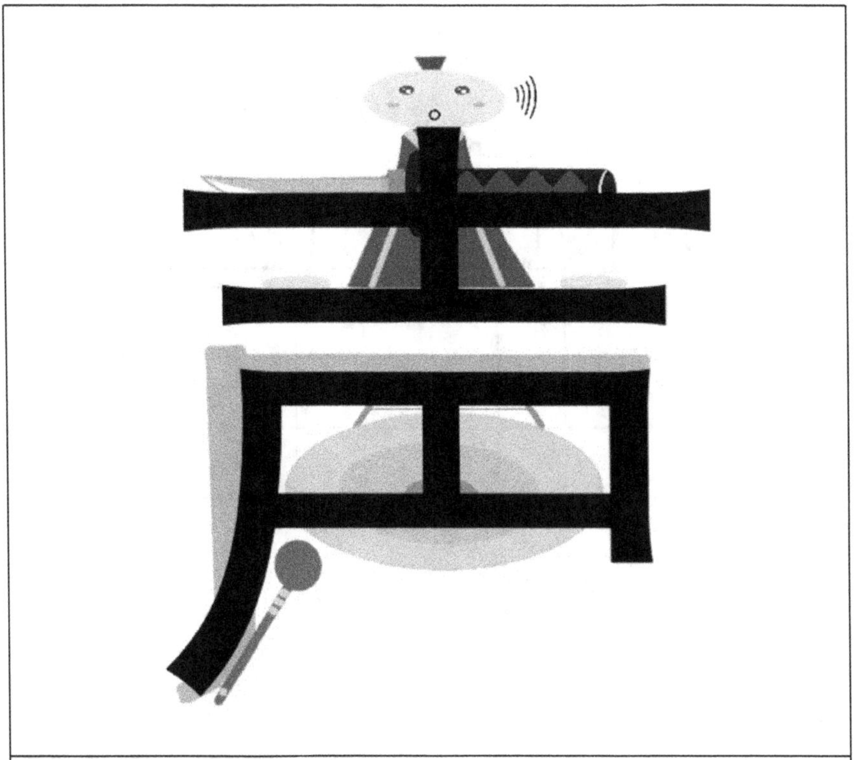

声 VOICE

"The voice (声) of the samurai (士) and the musical instruments resound"

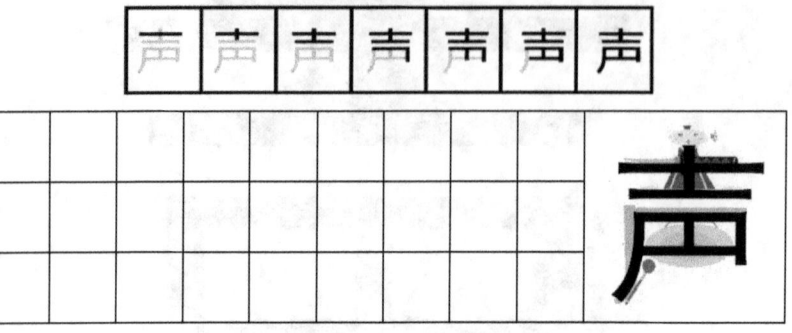

Kun (こえ)

こえ
声: Voice

*The original kanji was 聲, which also included a hand and an ear.

首 NECK

"A man with a long neck (首)"

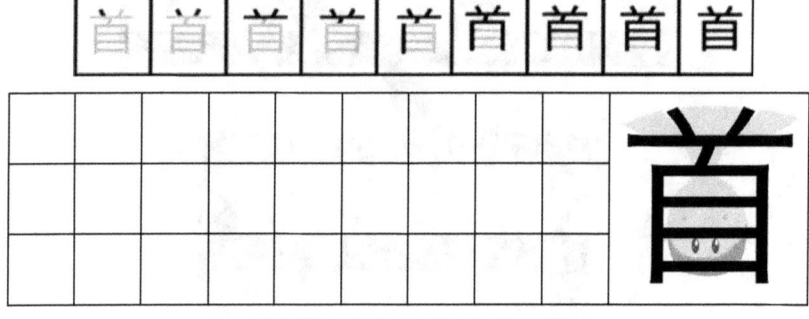

Kun (くび)

くび
首: Neck

頭 HEAD

"Your head (頭/頁) has the shape of a bean (豆)!"

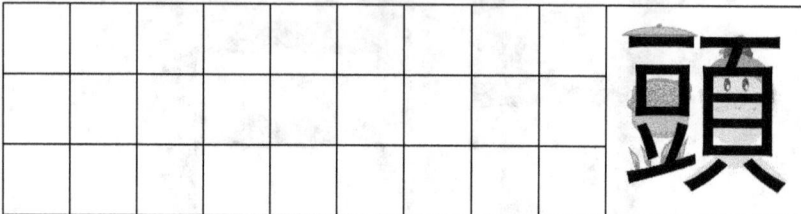

Kun (あたま)

あたま
頭 : Head

顔 FACE

"The boy uses a towel to clean his face (顔) and head (頁)"

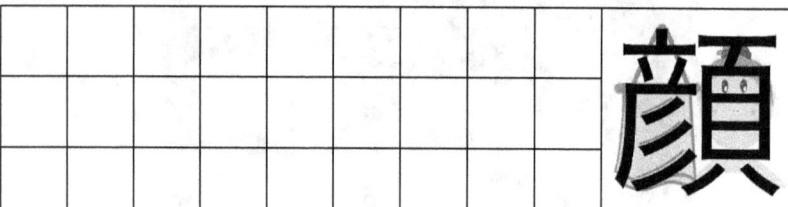

Kun (かお)

かお
顔: Face

*This kanji originally was the handsome face of a man.

CHAPTER 4: OBJECTS

物	事	品	台
35	36	37	38
図	画	服	紙
39	40	41	42

物 OBJECT, THING

"The cow (牛) catcher is a thing (物) mounted at the front of a locomotive"

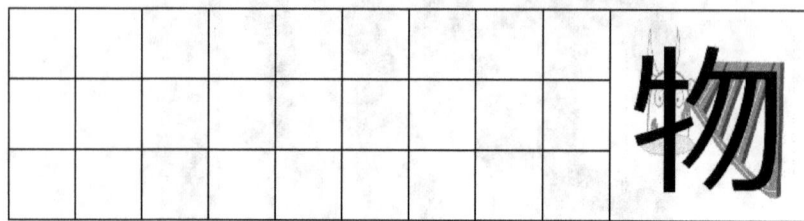

ON (ブツ, モツ)	Kun (もの)	
どうぶつ 動物: Animal	か　もの 買い物: Shopping	くだもの 果物: Fruit
けんぶつ 見物: Sightseeing	の　もの 飲み物: Drink	たてもの 建物: Building
にもつ 荷物: Luggage	た　もの 食べ物: Food	もの 物: Thing

事 MATTER, THING

"I pierced a fish's mouth (口) with a thing (事) that looks like a hook (亅)"

ON (ジ)		Kun (こと)
へんじ 返事: Reply	だいじ 大事: Important	しごと 仕事: Job
じこ 事故: Accident	かじ 火事: Fire	こと 事: Matter
じむしょ 事務所: Office	ようじ 用事: Tasks	

品 GOODS

"I got a hold of some expensive goods (品) including these containers with wide mouths (口)"

ON (ヒン)	Kun (しな)
しょくりょうひん 食料品 : Groceries	しなもの 品物 : Goods

台 PEDESTAL

"I (ム) am behind the pedestal (台) getting ready for the opening (口) ceremony"

ON (タイ, ダイ)	
たいふう 台風 : Typhoon	だいどころ 台所 : Kitchen

*Originally this kanji meant "to begin fieldwork" and had no relationship to a pedestal.

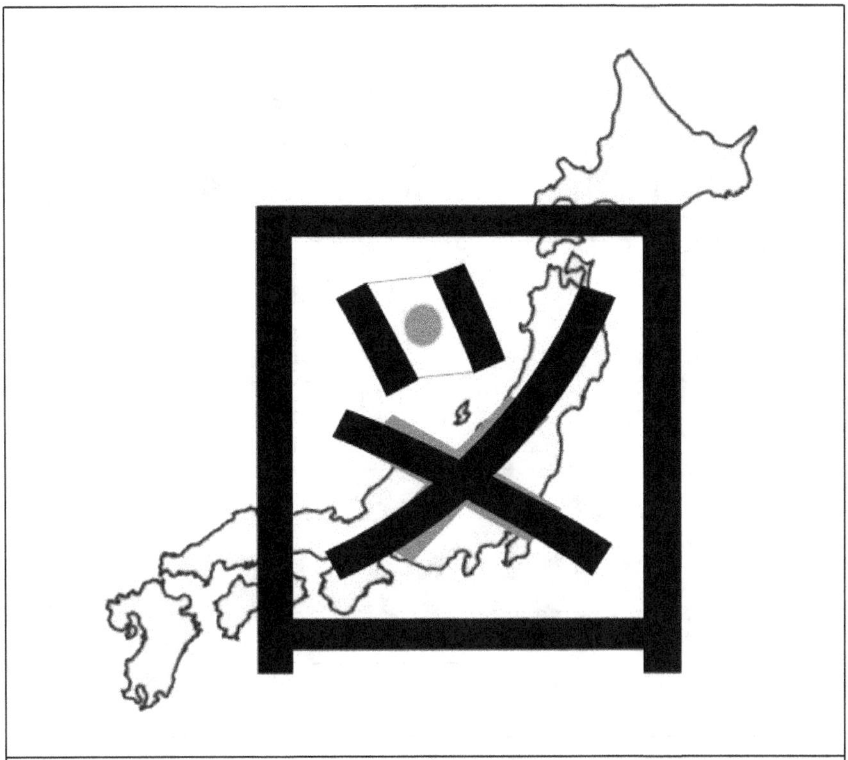

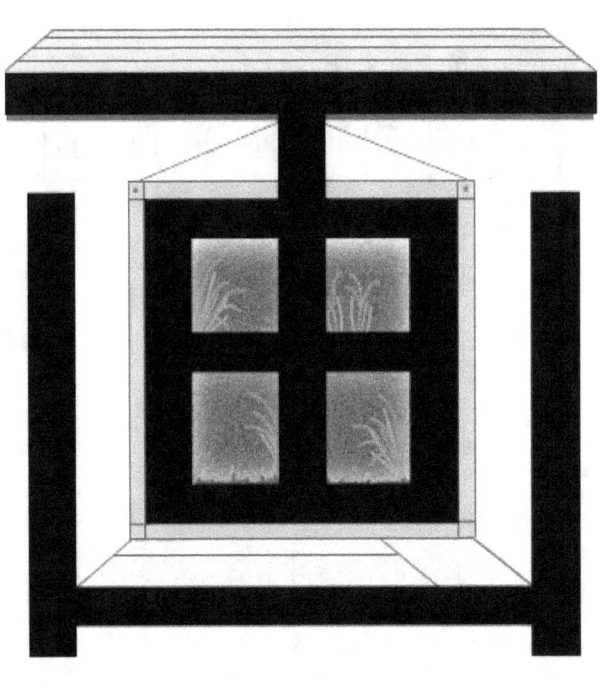

図 MAP

"Every map (図) has an enclosure (口) to show a specific area"

ON (ズ、ト)

ちず
地図: Map

としょかん
図書館: Library

画 PICTURE

"The hanging picture (画) is of a nearby rice field (田)"

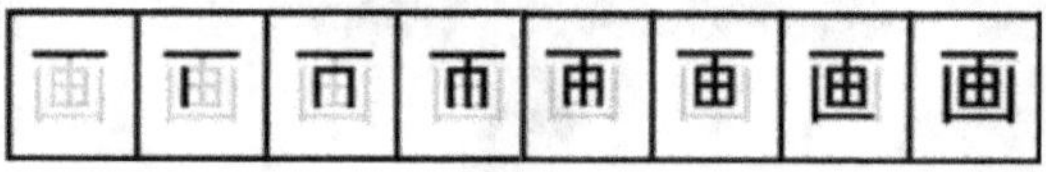

ON (ガ、カク)

えいが
映画: Movie

えいがかん
映画館: Cinema

まんが
漫画: Comic

けいかく
計画: Plan

服 CLOTHING

"He grabs a piece of clothing (服) with his hand (又) to fully cover his body (月)"

ON (フク)

服 (ふく): Clothing
洋服 (ようふく): Western-style clothes

紙 PAPER

"My family (氏) makes paper (紙) out of silk threads (糸)"

Kun (かみ)

紙 (かみ): Paper
手紙 (てがみ): Letter

CHAPTER 5: PEOPLE

私	自	方	族
43	44	45	46
姉	妹	兄	弟
47	48	49	50
親	主	員	民
51	52	53	54
医	者		
55	56		

私 I, ME

"I (私/ム) will be the one to collect the grains (禾)"

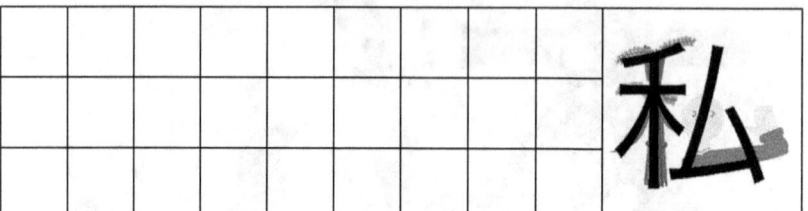

Kun (わたし, わたくし)

私(わたし) : I, me

私(わたくし) : (Humble) I, me

自 ONESELF

"I'm pointing at myself (自)"

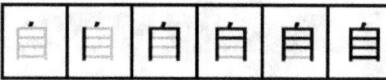

ON (ジ)

自分(じぶん): Oneself

自転車(じてんしゃ): Bicycle

自動車(じどうしゃ): Automobile

自由(じゆう): Freedom

方 PERSON, DIRECTION

"That person is indicating the correct direction (方)"

ON (ホウ)	Kun (かた, がた)	
りょうほう 両方 : Both sides	ゆうがた 夕方 : Evening しかた 仕方 : Method	かた 方 : Direction, person およ かた 泳ぎ方 : Way of swimming

*The kanji was originally a hoe with a handle pointing at all directions.

族 FAMILY

"In the past, families (族) weren't just related by blood. They also fought together shooting arrows (矢) while carrying their clan's flag pole (㫃)"

ON (ゾク)
かぞく 家族: Family

姉 ELDER SISTER

"The elder sister (姉) loves to be out in the city (市) without her female (女) friends"

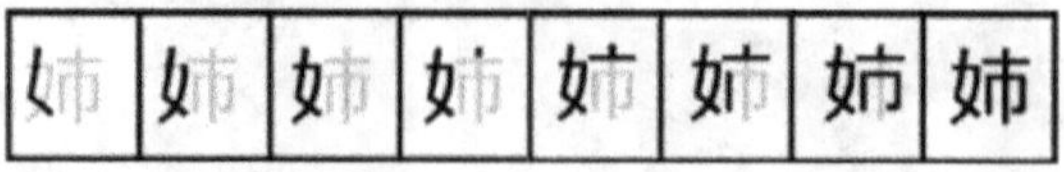

Kun (あね)

姉 (あね): Older sister
お姉さん (ねえ): (Honorable) older sister

妹 YOUNGER SISTER

"My younger sister (妹) is not yet (未) ready to visit the city without her female (女) friends"

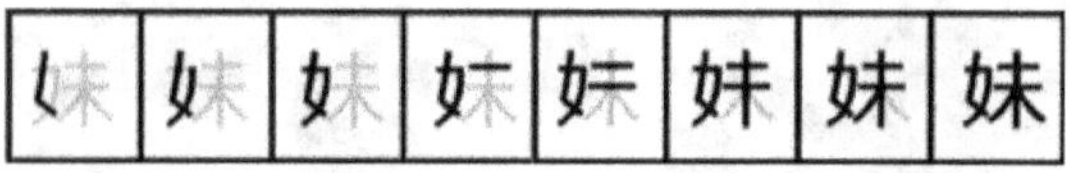

Kun (いもうと)

妹 (いもうと): Younger sister

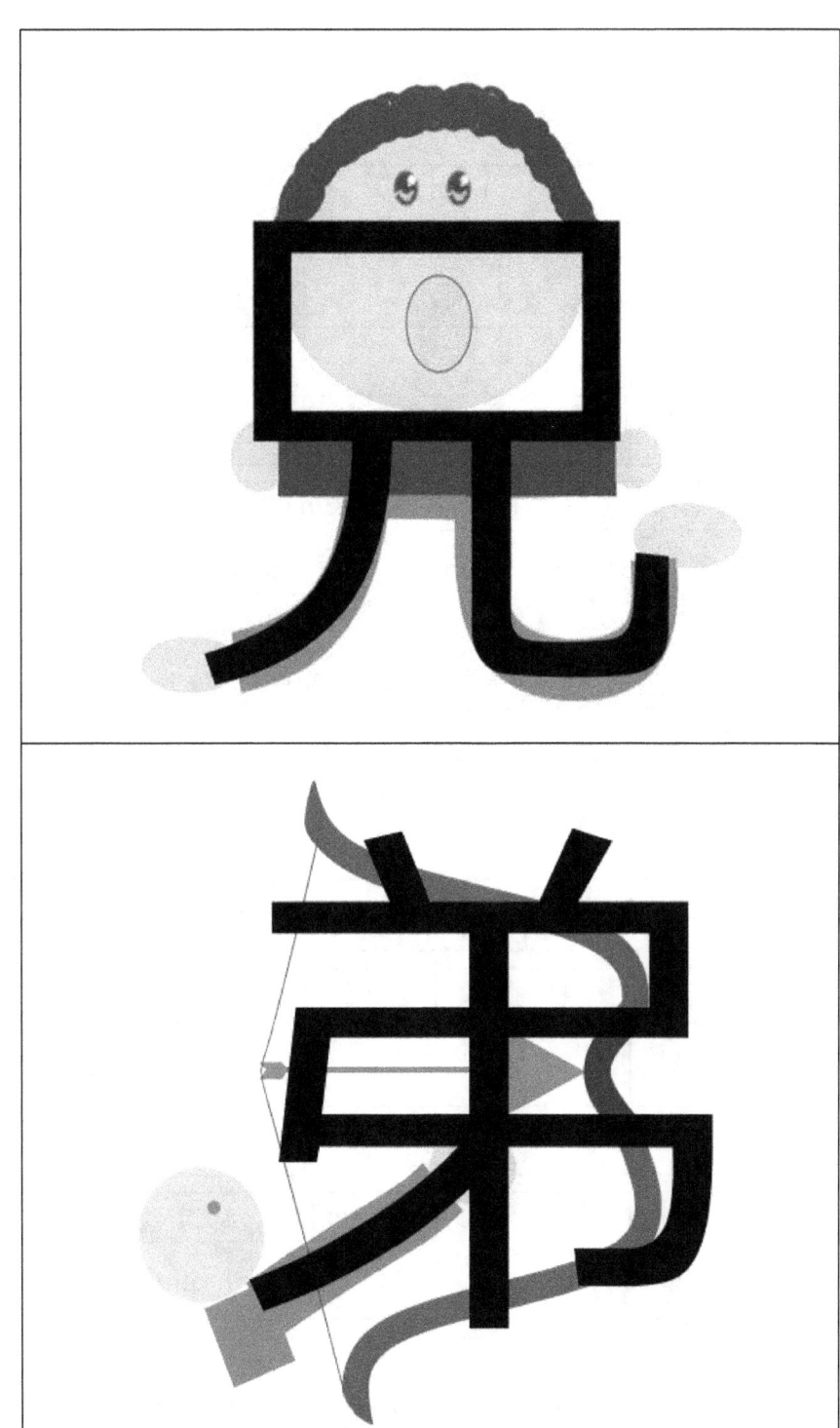

兄 ELDER BROTHER

"The elder brother (兄) has long legs (儿) and a big mouth (口)"

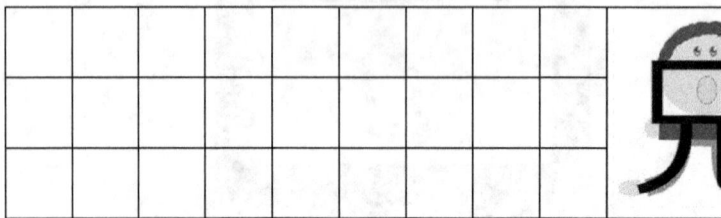

ON (キョウ)	Kun (あに)
きょうだい 兄弟 : Siblings	あに 兄 : Elder brother にい お兄さん: (Honorable) older brother

弟 YOUNGER BROTHER

"My younger brother (弟) is an expert at using the bow (弓)"

ON (ダイ)	Kun (おとうと)
きょうだい 兄弟 : Siblings	おとうと 弟 : Younger brother

*This kanji was originally a stake wrapped by a strap with something at the end. That something was the compared to a younger brother, who essentially was lower than the rest.

親 PARENT, RELATIVE

"I used to see (見) my parents (親) as bitter (辛) human beings"

ON (シン)		Kun (おや)
りょうしん 両親: Both parents	しんせつ 親切: Kindness	おや 親: Parents

*The radical for bitter came from a tattoing needle that was used on criminals.

主 CHIEF

"The king (王) has a crown; the Indian chief (主) has a feather headdress"

ON (シュ)
しゅじん ご主人: (honorable) your husband

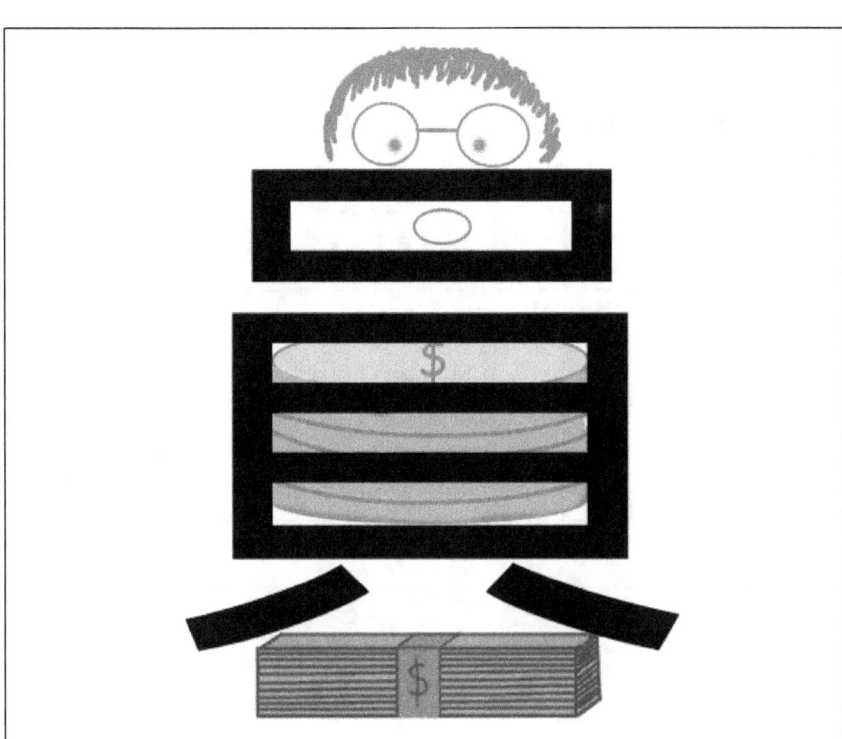
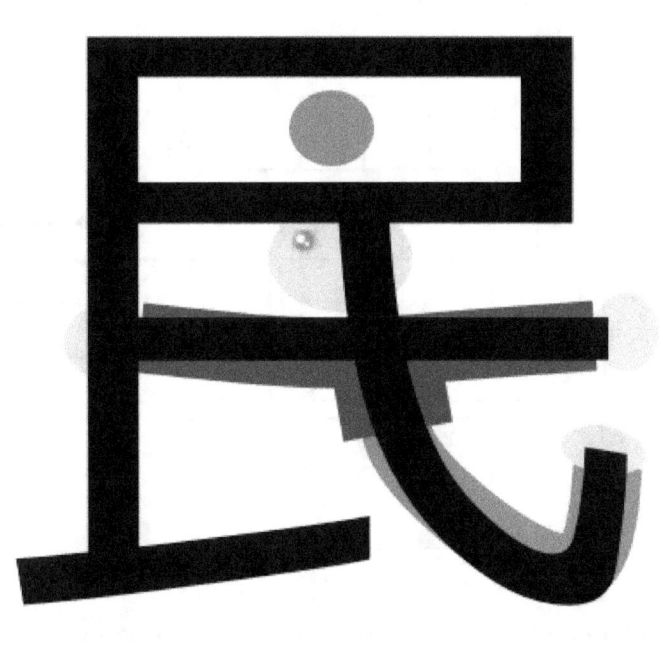

員 EMPLOYEE, MEMBER

"The employee (員) opens his mouth (口) of surprise after receiving more money (貝) than he expected"

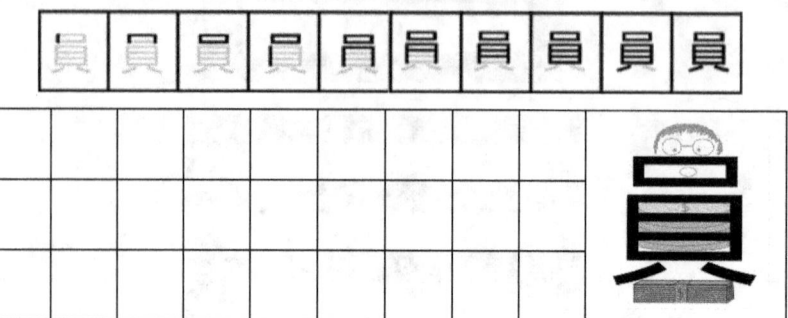

ON (イン)

こうむいん 公務員: Civil servant	てんいん 店員: Shop assistant いん ～員: Member of~

民 PEOPLE, NATION

"The family (氏) carries the flag from their nation (民)"

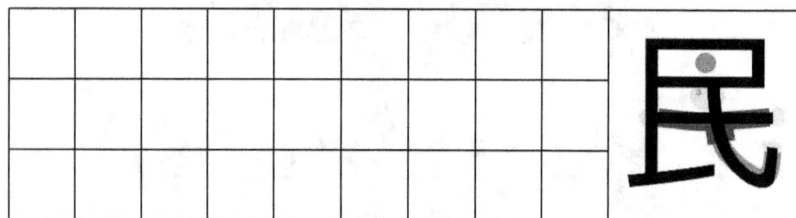

ON (ミン)

しみん
市民: Citizen

*The original kanji came from an eye with a needle piercing the eye to make them blind. It made reference to people following their ruler blindly.

医 DOCTOR, MEDICINE

"The doctor (医) has removed the arrow (矢) from the wounded warrior"

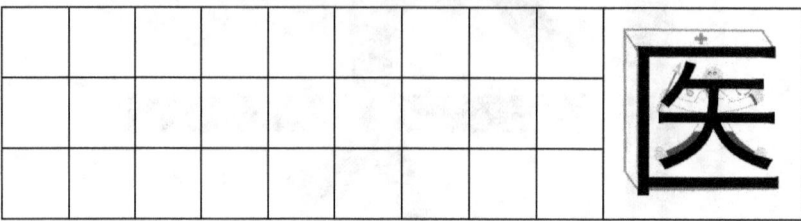

ON (イ)

医者: Medical doctor (いしゃ)
医学: Medical science (いがく)

歯医者: Dentist (はいしゃ)

者 SOMEONE, PERSON

"She is someone (者) who may be old (耂), but still loves to be sitting in the sun (日)"

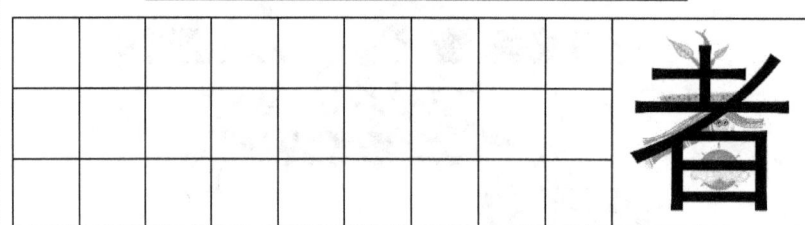

ON (シャ)

医者: Medical doctor (いしゃ)
歯医者: Dentist (はいしゃ)

Kun (もの)

者: Person (もの)

CHAPTER 6: PLACES

場	所	屋	室	家	門
57	58	59	60	61	62
院	館	工	堂	村	町
63	64	65	66	67	68
市	洋	区	県	都	京
69	70	71	72	73	74
漢	英	世	界		
75	76	77	78		

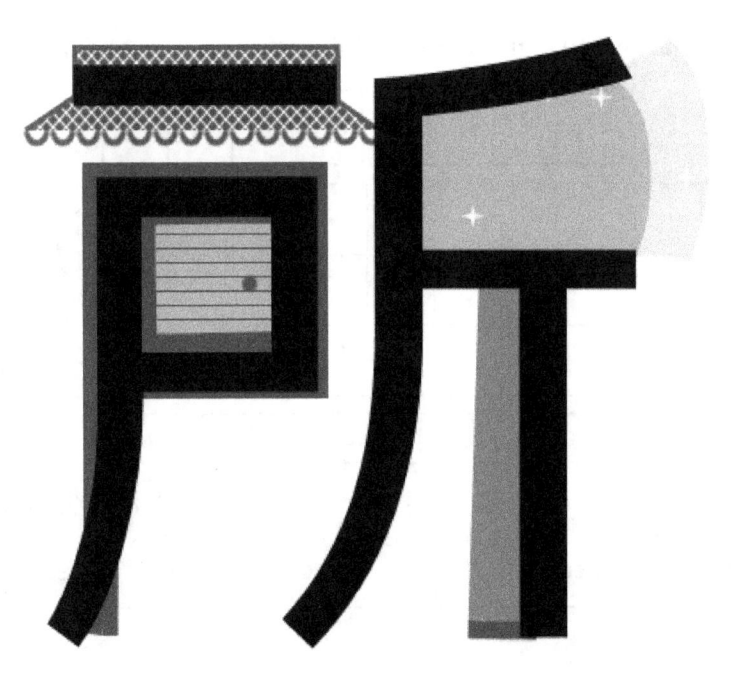

場 PLACE

"The sun rays (昜) shine above that place (場) full of plants (土)"

場 場 場 場 場 場 場 場 場 場 場 場

ON (ジョウ)

にゅうじょう
入場: Entrance, admission

かいじょう
会場: Assembly hall

ひこうじょう
飛行場: Airport

Kun (ば)

ばしょ
場所: Location

ばあい
場合: Situation

う　ば
売り場: Point of sale

所 PLACE

"That place (所) with the closed door (戸) has an axe (斤) inside"

所 所 所 所 所 所 所 所 所

ON (ショ)

きんじょ
近所: Neighborhood

じむしょ
事務所: Office

じゅうしょ
住所: Address

ばしょ
場所: Location

Kun (ところ)

だいどころ
台所: Kitchen

ところ
所: Place, spot

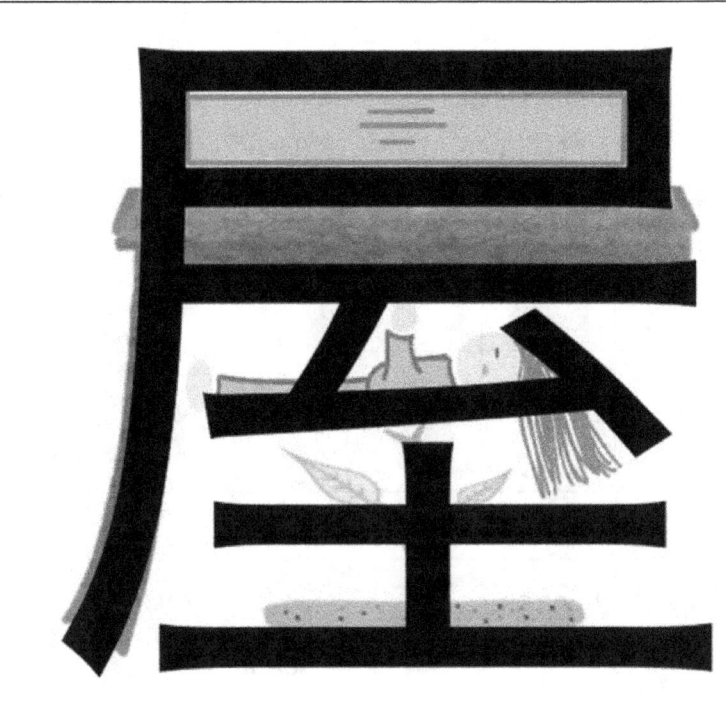

屋 ROOF, HOUSE

"So tired that I'm feeling like a corpse (尸)! Can't wait to arrive (至) to my house (屋) and rest"

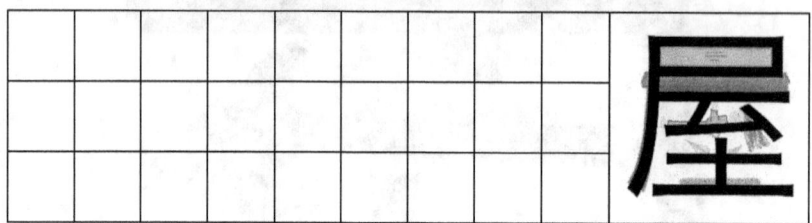

ON (オク)	Kun (や)
おくじょう 屋上 : Rooftop	やおや 八百屋 : Greengrocer へや 部屋 : Room

室 ROOM, APARTMENT

"I just arrived (至) to the apartment (室) with a nice roof (宀)"

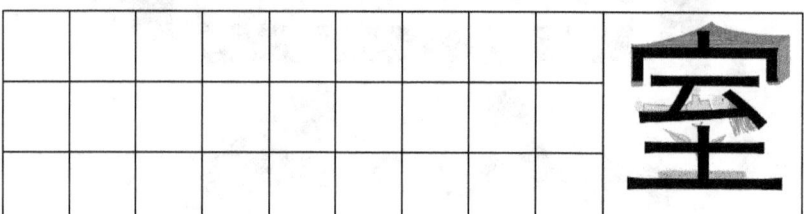

ON (シツ)
きょうしつ 教室 : Classroom けんきゅうしつ 研究室 : Study room, laboratory かいぎしつ 会議室 : Meeting room

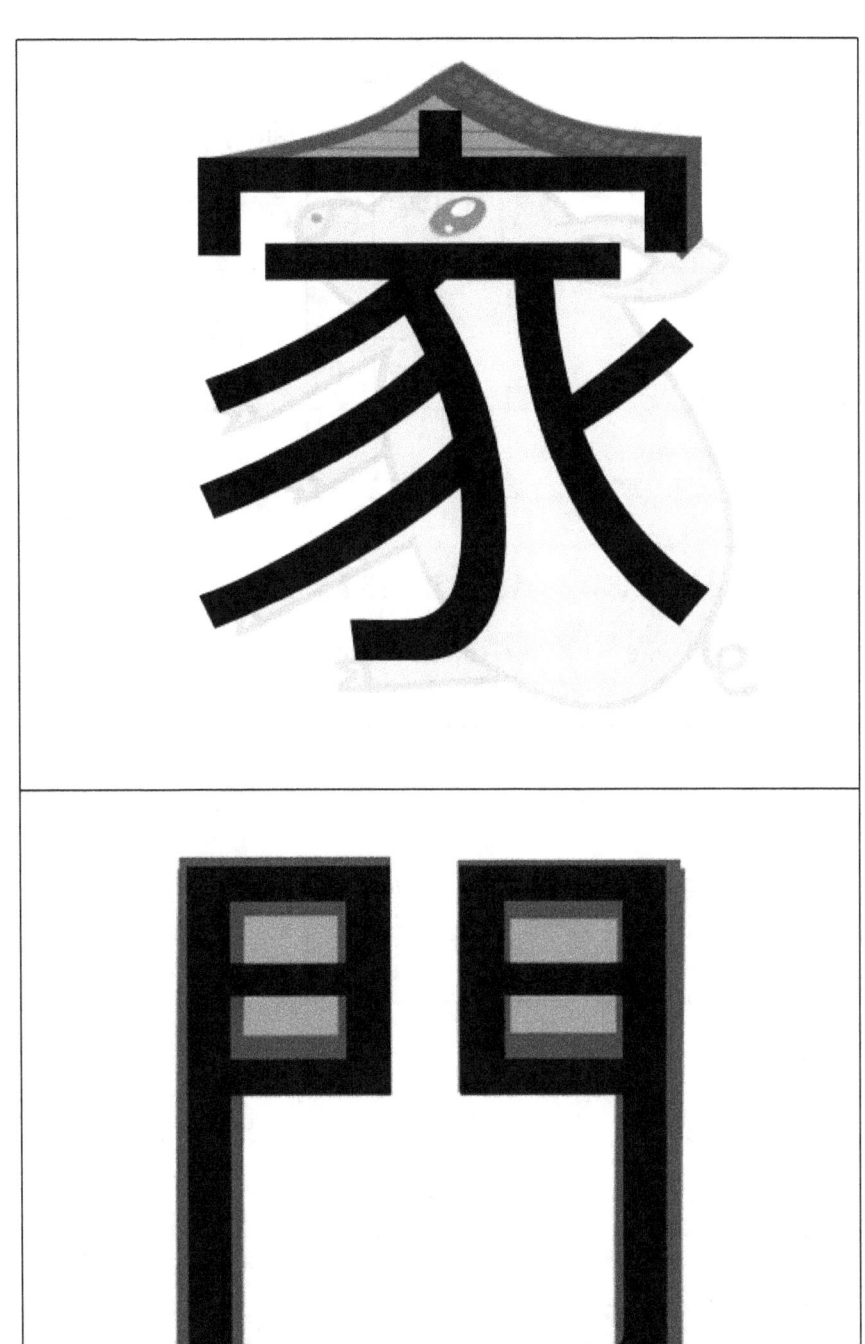

家 HOUSE, FAMILY

"That pig (豕) under the roof (宀) is like family (家) to me"

ON (カ)		Kun (いえ)
か て い 家庭: Household	か 〜家: Professional	いえ 家: House
か な い 家内: (my) wife	か ぞ く 家族: Family	

門 GATE

"The castle's gate (門) is right in front of you"

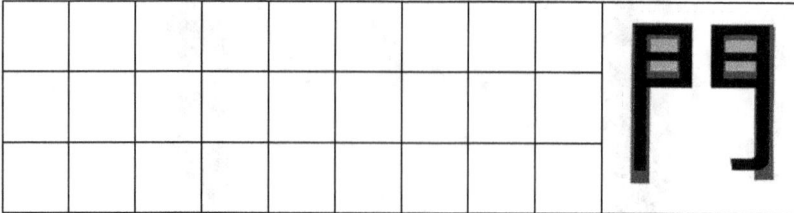

ON (モン)
もん 門: Gate

院 INSTITUTION

"The institution (院) next to the hill (阝) isn't perfect (完), but it fits me just right"

院 阝 阝 院 阝 院 院 院 院 院 院

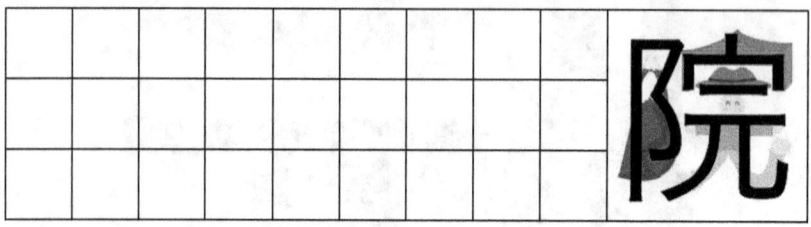

ON (イン)

にゅういん
入院: To hospitalize

びょういん
病院: Hospital

たいいん
退院: To leave hospital

館 BUILDING, MANSION

"The large mansion (館), which belongs to the government (官), always has a lot of food (食)"

館 館 館 館 館 館 館
館 館 館 館 館 館 館 館

ON (カン)

たいしかん
大使館: Embassy

りょかん
旅館: Japanese hotel

えいがかん
映画館: Cinema

としょかん
図書館: Library

びじゅつかん
美術館: Art gallery

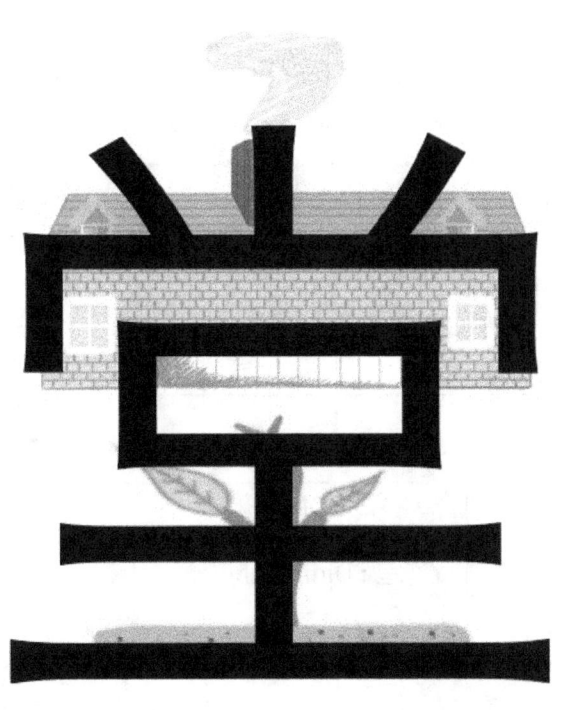

工 CONSTRUCTION

"Different types of tools are used at construction (工) sites"

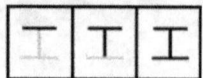

ON (コウ)	
こうば 工場: Factory	こうぎょう 工業: (Manufacturing) industry
こうじょう 工場: Factory	

堂 HALL

"That is a very high status (尚) hall (堂) built with a high-quality soil (土) for supporting foundation"

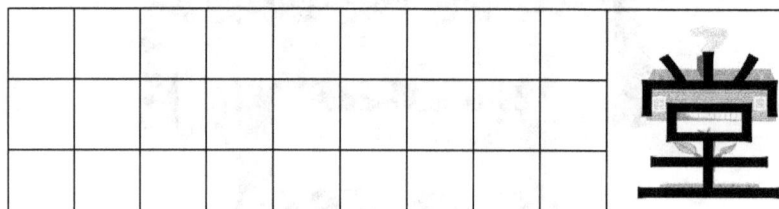

ON (ドウ)
しょくどう 食堂: Dining hall
こうどう 講堂: Auditorium

村 VILLAGE

"The area measurement (寸) of this village (村) is so small that it only has one tree (木)"

村 村 村 村 村 村 村

Kun (むら)
む ら 村: Village

町 TOWN

"The town (町) has a small rice field (田) and just one street (丁)"

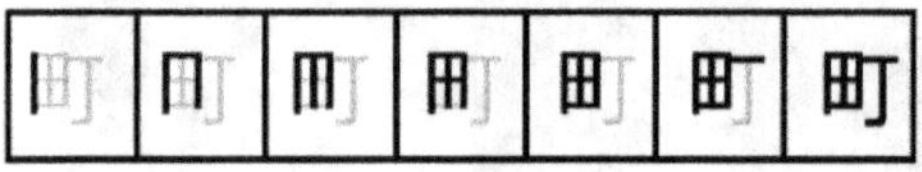

町 町 町 町 町 町 町

ON (チョウ)	Kun (まち)
ちょう 〜 町 : 〜 Of the town	まち 町: Town, block

市 CITY

"This is the city (市) that has tall buildings with hanging scrolls (巾)"

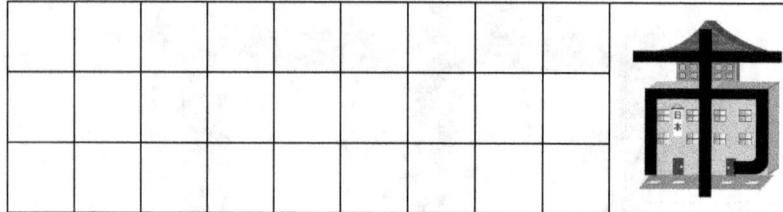

ON (シ)

市: City
市民: Citizen

洋 OCEAN, WESTERN STYLE

"The sheep (羊) plays with the water (氵) of the ocean (洋)"

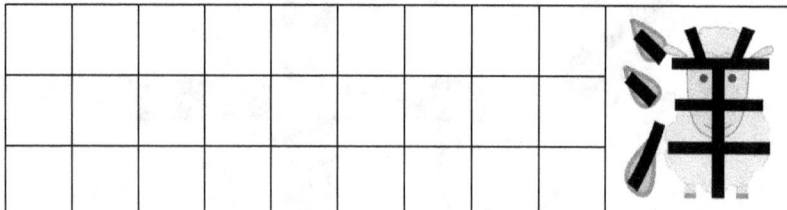

ON (ヨウ)

西洋: Western countries
洋服: Western-style clothes

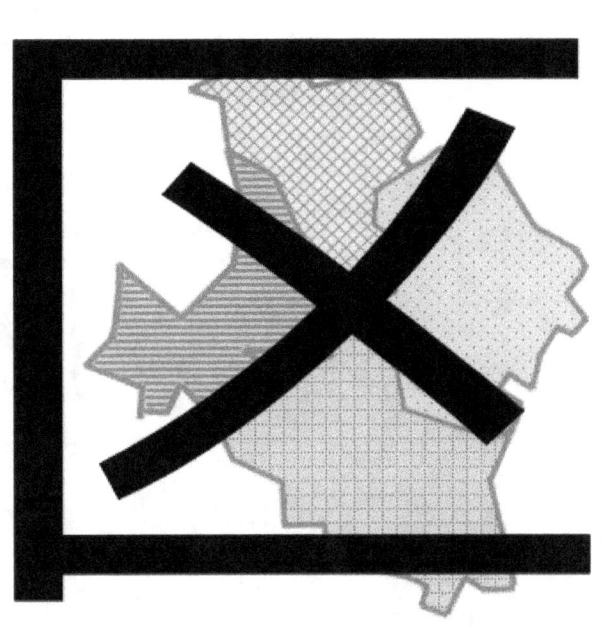

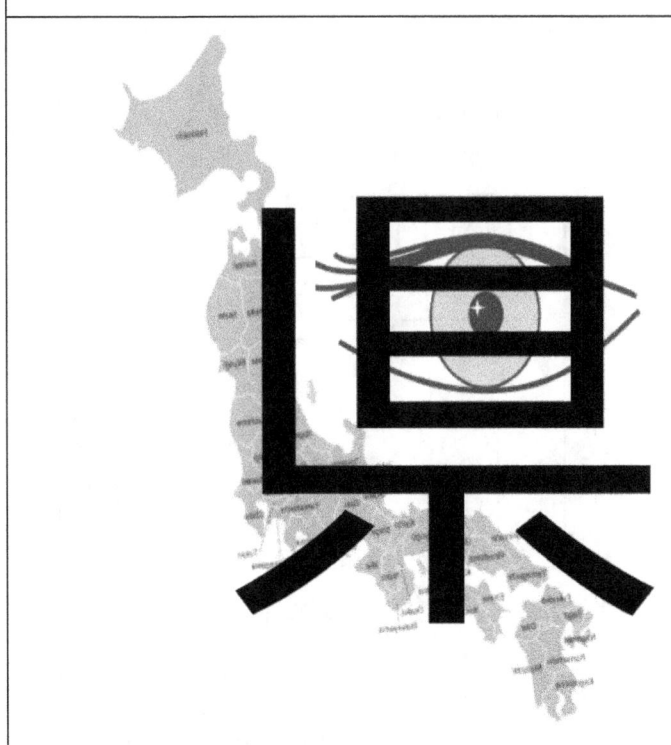

区 DISTRICT

"You can clearly see the enclosure (匚) showing four districts (区) in Tokyo"

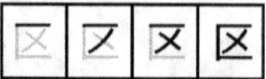

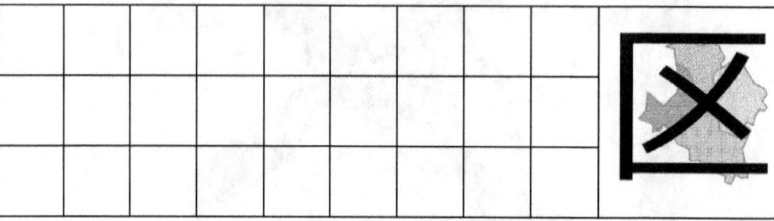

ON (ク)

区別: Distinction 地区: District	～区: District of ～

県 PREFECTURE

"Prefectures are smaller (小) to the eye (目) compared to the whole country"

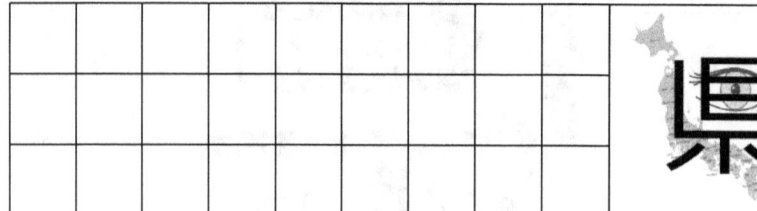

ON (ケン)

県: Prefecture

*The original kanji was the head of a criminal hanging. The current kanji is just a simplification.

都 METROPOLIS, CAPITAL

"A person (者) who likes the city (阝) can easily live in the capital (都)"

| 都 | 都 | 都 | 者 | 者 | 者 | 者 | 者 | 都 | 都 | 都 |

ON (ト, ツ)

都合 (つごう): Circumstances
都 (と): Metropolitan

京 CAPITAL

"The small (小) girl is in front of the capital's (京) tallest building"

| 京 | 京 | 京 | 京 | 京 | 京 | 京 | 京 |

ON (キョウ)

東京 (とうきょう): Tokyo
上京 (じょうきょう): Proceeding to the capital (Tokyo)

漢 CHINA

"China (漢) is a big (大) country with a lot plants (艹) and water (氵)"

ON (カン)

<ruby>漢字<rt>かんじ</rt></ruby>: Chinese character

英 ENGLAND, ENGLISH

"The prime meridian at Greenwich, England (英), became the center (央) land (艹) of the world time"

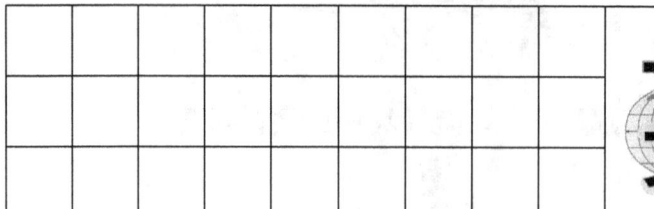

ON (エイ)

<ruby>英語<rt>えいご</rt></ruby>: English language

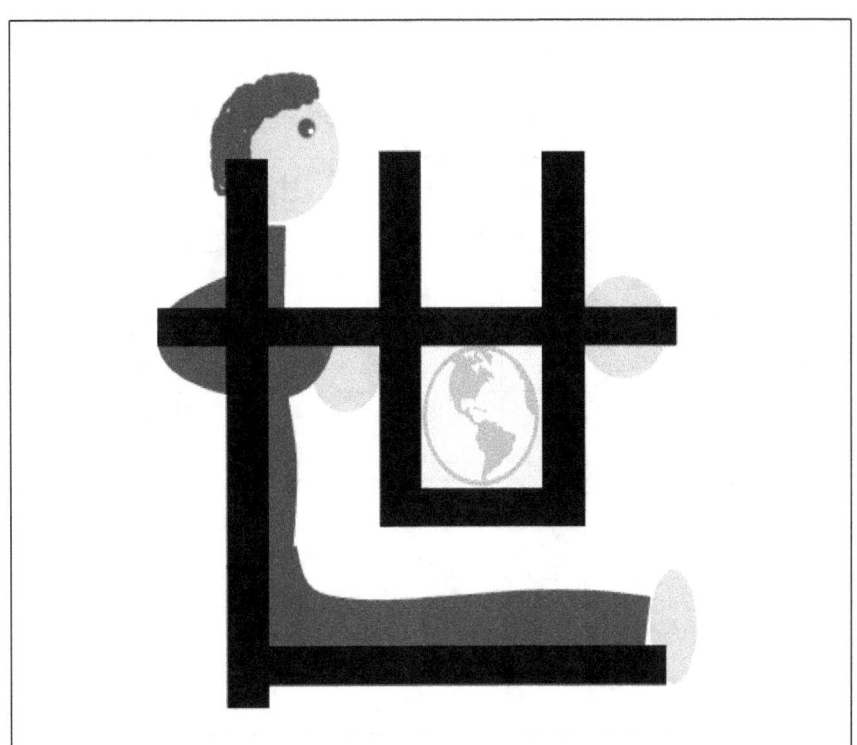

世 WORLD, SOCIETY

"One (一) man is holding a world (世) map"

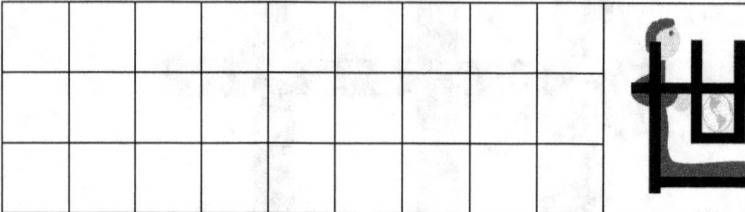

ON (セ)

世界: World
世話: Looking after

界 WORLD, BOUNDARY

"This world (界) has nice rice fields (田) but it also has places jammed in (介) with people"

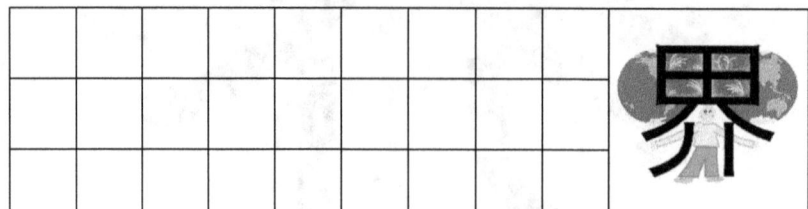

ON (カイ)

世界: World

CHAPTER 7: ADJECTIVES

明	暗	青	赤	黒	便
79	80	81	82	83	84
重	軽	遠	近	弱	強
85	86	87	88	89	90
正	悪	短	低	太	広
91	92	93	94	95	96
		寒	暑		
		97	98		

明 BRIGHT

"The moon (月) is not as bright (明) as the sun (日)"

明	明	明	明	明	明	明	明

ON (メイ)	Kun (あ, あか)
<ruby>説明<rt>せつめい</rt></ruby>: Explanation	<ruby>明日<rt>あした</rt></ruby>: Tomorrow <ruby>明日<rt>あす</rt></ruby>: Tomorrow <ruby>明<rt>あか</rt></ruby>るい: Bright

暗 DARKNESS, SHADE

"He prefers to be a in a place of darkness (暗) and no sound (音)"

暗	暗	暗	暗	暗	暗
暗	暗	暗	暗	暗	暗

Kun (くら)
<ruby>暗<rt>くら</rt></ruby>い: Dark, gloomy

青 BLUE

"In this picture, you can see pretty plants (龶), a blue (青) sky, and a beautiful moon (月)"

青 青 青 青 青 青 青 青

Kun (あお)
^{あお}青い: (adj) Blue
^{あお}青: (n) Blue

赤 RED

"His face is so red (赤) after burning plants (土) with fire"

赤 赤 赤 赤 赤 赤 赤

Kun (あか)
^{あか}赤い: (adj) Red
^{あか}赤ん^{ぼう}坊: Baby
^{あか}赤: (n) Red

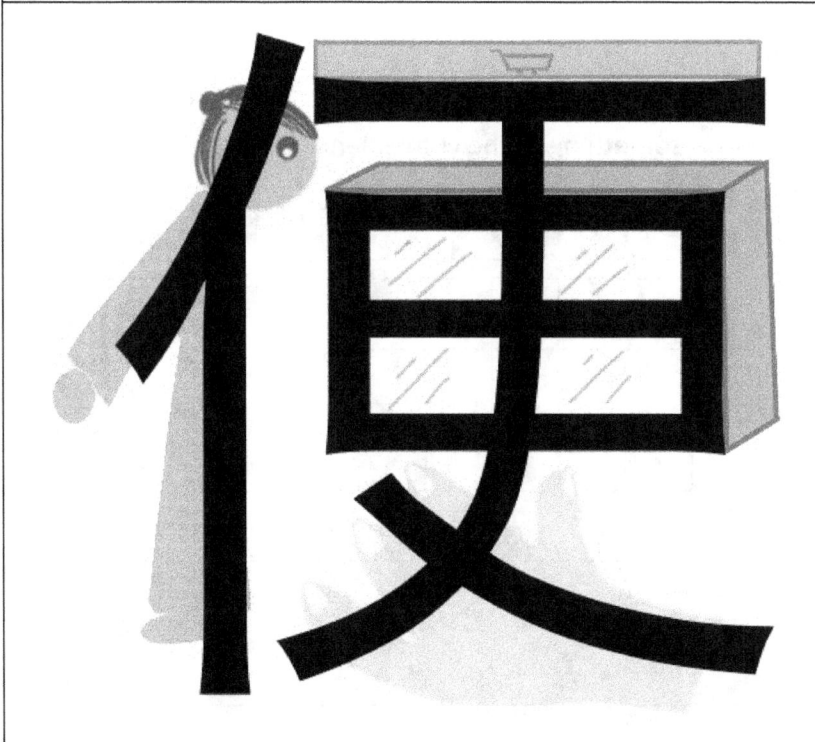

黒 BLACK

"The fire (灬) burned down the whole village (里) and now everything is black (黒) ashes"

黒 黒 黒 黒 黒 黒
黒 黒 黒 黒 黒

Kun (くろ)

黒い: (adj) Black	黒: (n) Black

便 CONVENIENCE

"It is getting too late (更) for that person (亻) to go grab something at the convenience (便) store"

便 便 便 便 便 便 便 便 便

ON (ベン, ビン)

便利: Useful	郵便局: Post office
不便: Inconvenience	

重 HEAVY

"One person in this village (里) can lift up heavy (重) weights"

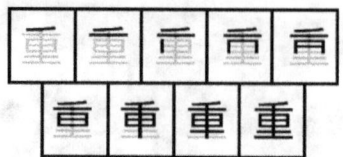

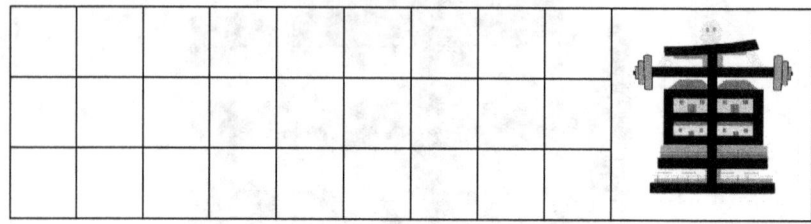

Kun (おも)
おも 重い: Heavy

*This kanji was originally a heavy bag that was tied.

軽 LIGHTLY

"That car (車) on the ground (土) is so light (軽), it can be lifted with one hand (又)"

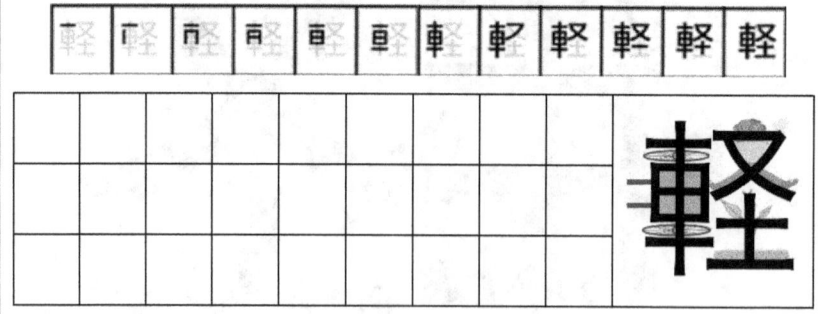

Kun (かる)
かる 軽い: Light (not heavy)

*The original kanji (輕) was a military vehicle that was not carrying heavy equipment.

遠 DISTANT, FAR

"The girl with pretty clothes (衣) takes the longest road (辶) and goes in a far (遠) away journey"

ON (エン)	Kun (とお)	
^{えんりょ}遠慮: To be reserved	^{とお}遠い: (adj) Far	^{とお}遠く: (n) Far

*Originally this kanji signified sending the deceased in a far away journey.

近 NEAR

"The axe (斤) is near (近) the road (辶)"

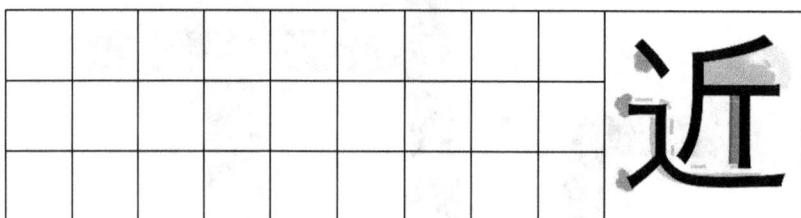

ON (キン)	Kun (ちか)
^{きんじょ}近所: Neighborhood	^{ちか}近い: (adj) Near
^{さいきん}最近: Latest	^{ちか}近く: (n) Near

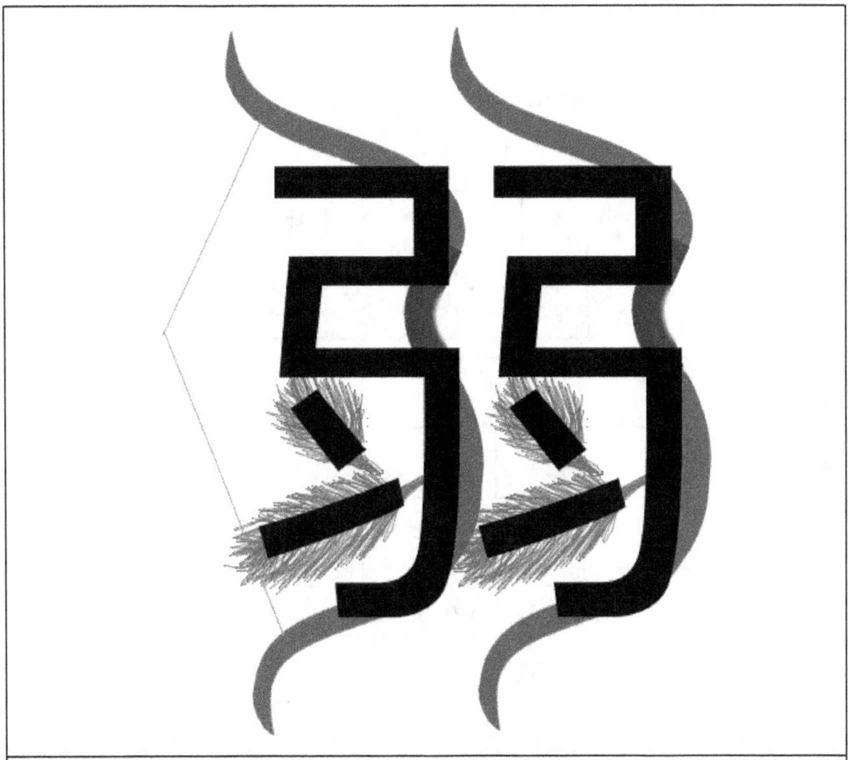

弱 WEAK

"The bow (弓) would be pretty weak (弱) if made out of feathers (羽)"

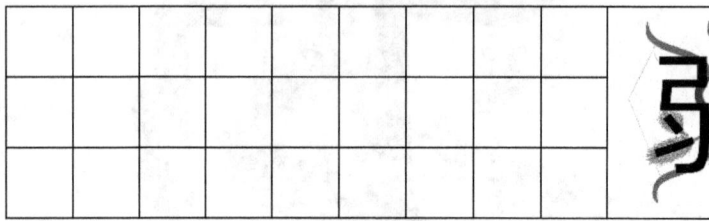

Kun (よわ)
よわ 弱い: Weak

強 STRONG

"I (ム) shall be strong (強) and use the bow (弓) to kill the big bug (虫)"

ON (キョウ)	Kun (つよ)
べんきょう 勉強: Study	つよ 強い: Strong

正 CORRECT, JUSTICE

"We should never stop (止) fighting for justice (正)"

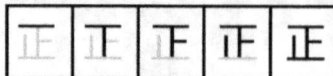

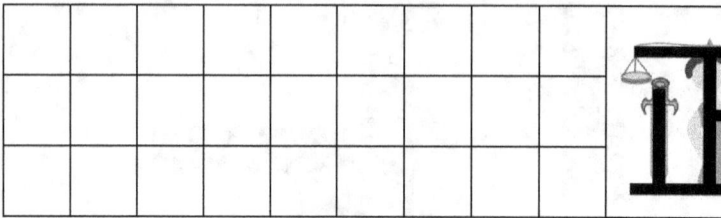

Kun (ただ)
ただ 正しい: Right, correct

*This kanji was originally a footpring headed to conquer a town. In the old times, conquering areas was just and correct.

悪 BAD, WRONG, EVIL

"It is so bad (悪) for my heart (心) that I don't have enough money to travel to Asia (亜)"

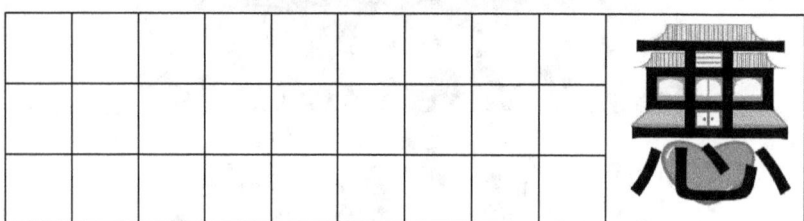

Kun (わる)
わる 悪い: Bad

短豆

低

短 SHORT, BREVITY

"She uses a short (短) arrow (矢) to mix the beans (豆)"

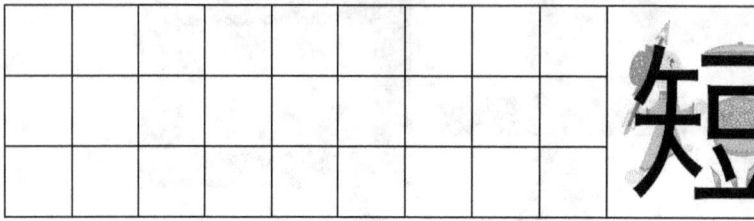

Kun (みじか)
短い: Short

低 LOWER, HUMBLE

"My family (氏) is of a lower (低) social status than that person (亻)"

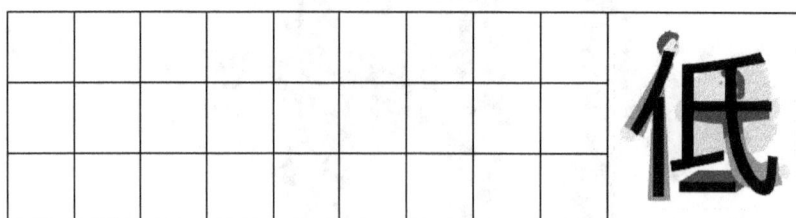

Kun (ひく)
低い: Low

太 PLUMP, THICK

"That man is quite big (大) and plump (太)"

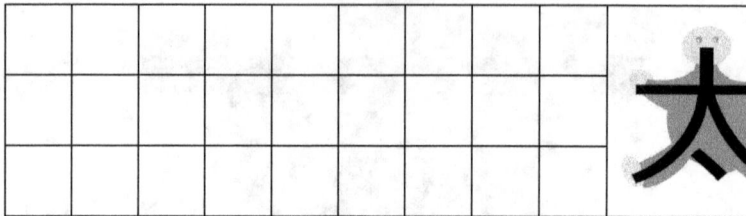

Kun (ふと)

太い: Fat
太る: To grow fat

広 WIDE, SPACIOUS

"This tent (广) is more spacious (広) than I (厶) thought"

Kun (ひろ)

広い: Spacious, wide
背広: Business suit

*The original kanji was a fire arrow, which when shot, it illuminated a wide area.

寒 COLD

"We are staying together (共) under a warm roof (宀) during this icy (冫) and cold (寒) weather"

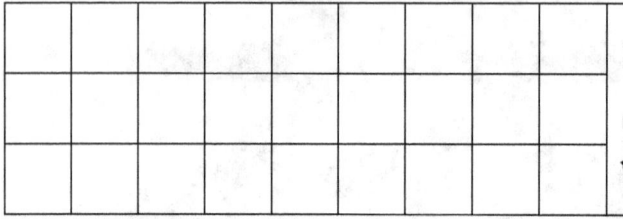

Kun (さむ)

寒い: Cold (weather)

暑 HOT

"Even on hot (暑) days, this old (耂) person (者) enjoys lying in the sun (日)"

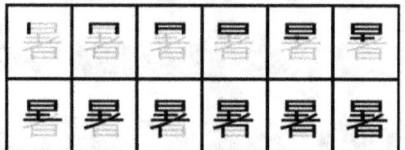
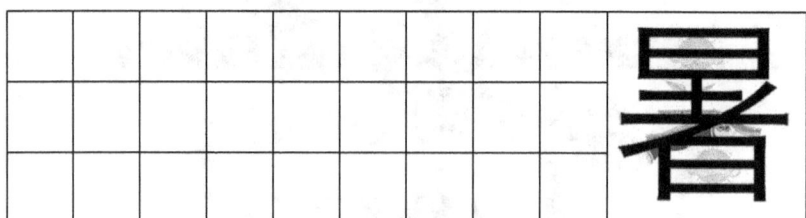

Kun (あつ)

暑い: Hot (weather)

CHAPTER 8: SPEECH

説	試	文	字	問	題
99	100	101	102	103	104

不	以	理	度
105	106	107	108

説 OPINION, EXPLANATION

"My older brother (兄) gives a speech (言) and an explanation (説) of his research"

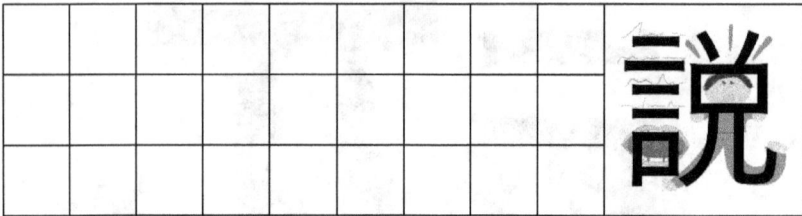

ON (セツ)	
しょうせつ 小説: Novel	せつめい 説明: Explanation

試 TEST, ATTEMPT

"He is making an attempt (試) to give a speech (言) about his work (工) during the ceremony (式)"

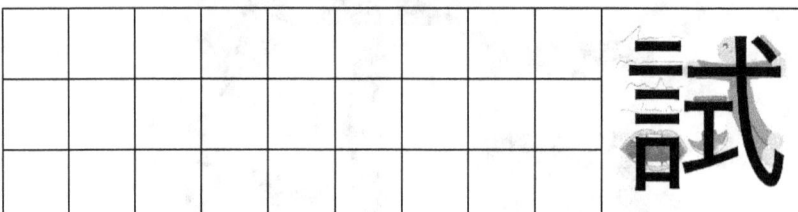

ON (シ)	
しあい 試合: Match, game	しけん 試験: Examination

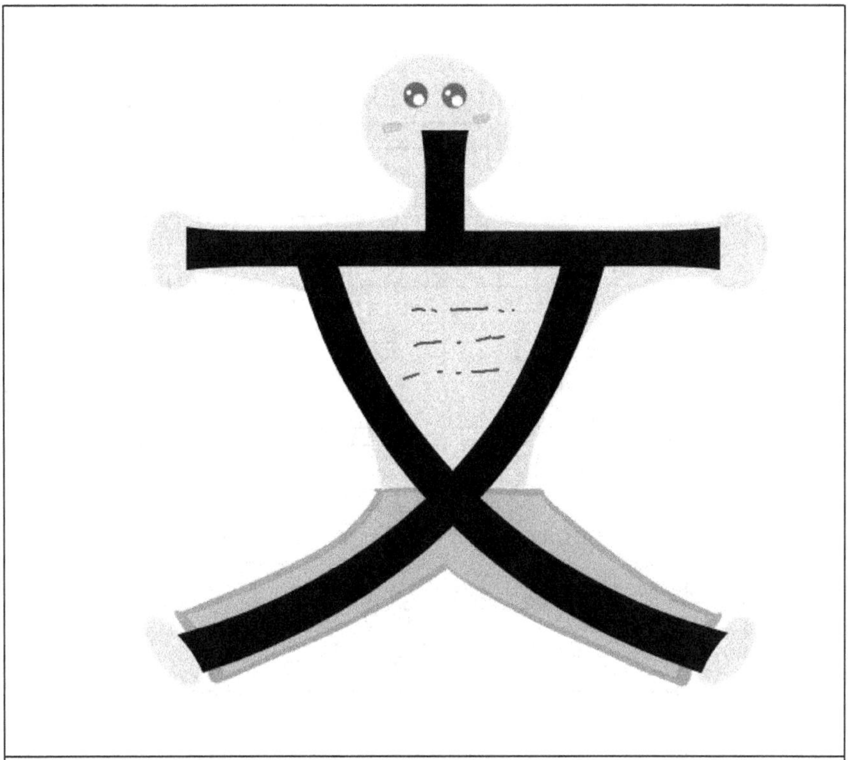

文 SENTENCE, LITERATURE

"The man has some sentences (文) tattooed on his chest"

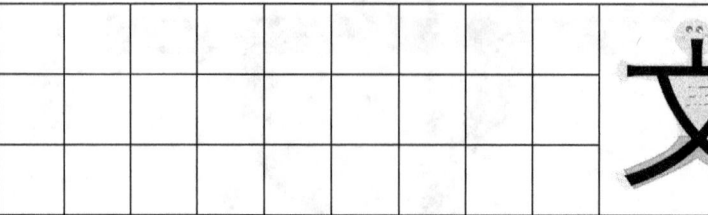

ON (ブン)

さくぶん 作文: Composition	ぶんしょう 文章: Sentence
ぶんがく 文学: Literature	ぶんか 文化: Culture
	ぶんぽう 文法: Grammar

字 CHARACTER, LETTER

"The child (子) learns the letters (字) at the school with the big roof (宀)"

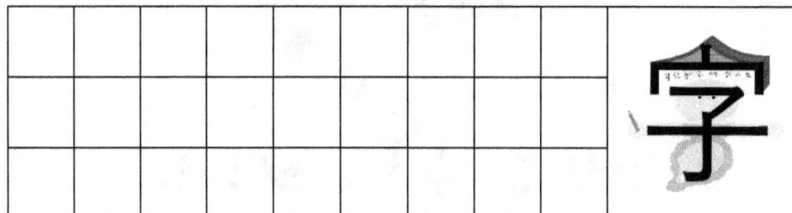

ON (ジ)

じびき 字引: Dictionary	かんじ 漢字: Chinese character
じ 字: Character	

問 QUESTION, PROBLEM

"The mouth (口) asks many questions (問) behind closed doors (門)"

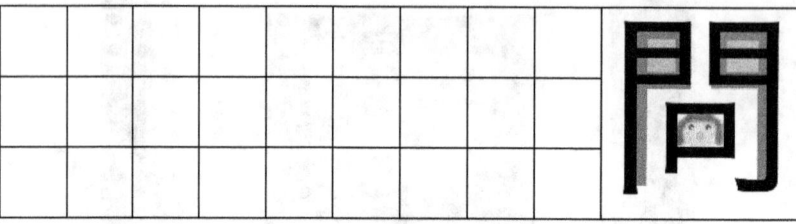

ON (モン)

| 学問: Study, Learning | 問題: Problem |
| 質問: Question | |

題 TOPIC, SUBJECT

"His head (頁) only thinks about topics (題) like law and justice (是)"

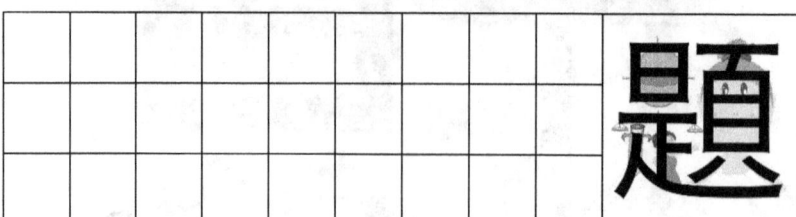

ON (ダイ)

| 問題: Problem | 宿題: Homework |

不 NEGATIVE

"He has a very negative (不) face"

| 不 | 不 | 不 | 不 |

ON (フ)

ふべん
不便: Inconvenience

*This kanji was originally the pictograph of a calyx of a flower. It was later borrowed to mean "negation".

以 BY MEANS OF, BECAUSE

"The person (人) works in the field by means of (以) different tools, including a hoe"

| 以 | 以 | 以 | 以 | 以 |

ON (イ)

いない
以内: Within

いじょう
以上: No less than, … and more

いがい
以外: Excepting

いか
以下: Not exceeding

理 LOGIC, REASON

"The king (王) rules over the village (里) with a lot of logic (理)"

理 理 理 理 理 理
理 理 理 理 理

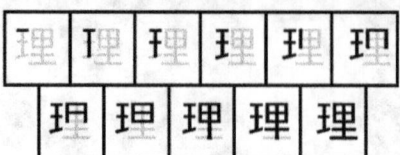

ON (リ)

りゆう 理由: Reason	ちり 地理: Geography
むり 無理: Impossible	りょうり 料理: Cooking

度 DEGREES, OCCURRENCE

"He must check if it is 70 degrees (度) inside the tent (广)"

度 度 度 度 度 度 度 度 度

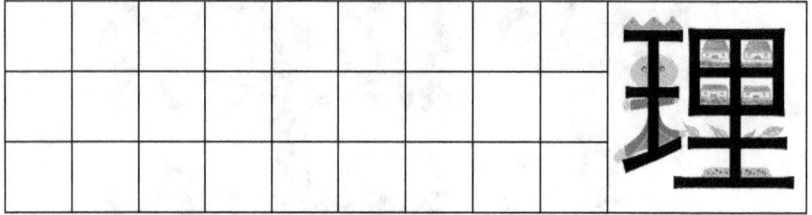

ON (ド、タク)

いちど 一度: Once	いちど もう一度: Once again
こんど 今度: Now, another time	したく 支度: To prepare

CHAPTER 9: ABSTRACT

音	意	楽	業	真	質
109	110	111	112	113	114
力	病	特	験	色	味
115	116	117	118	119	120
料	旅	元	同		
121	122	123	124		

音 SOUND, NOISE

"You must stand (立) up in the morning with the sound (音) of your alarm or the sun (日) rising"

| 音 | 音 | 音 | 音 | 音 | 音 | 音 | 音 | 音 |

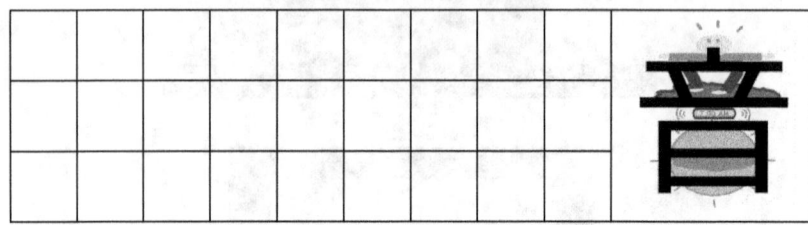

ON (オン)		Kun (おと)
^{おんがく} 音楽: Music	^{はつおん} 発音: Pronunciation	^{おと} 音: Sound

*What now looks like the radical of sun, it was a mouth with something inside, which signified sound.

意 IDEA, DESIRE

"My best ideas (意) come when I calm down and I hear the sound (音) of my heart (心)"

| 意 | 意 | 意 | 意 | 意 | 意 | 意 | 意 | 意 | 意 | 意 | 意 |

ON (イ)	
^{ようい} 用意: Preparation	^{ちゅうい} 注意: Caution
^{いけん} 意見: Opinion	^{いみ} 意味: Meaning

楽 MUSIC, CONFORT

"I often think there are white (白) angels playing music (楽) on top of trees (木)"

ON (ガク)	Kun (たの)	
おんがく 音楽: Music	たの 楽しみ: Enjoyment たの 楽しむ: To enjoy oneself	たの 楽しい: Enjoyable

*This kanji originally came from a musical instrument with ornamental threads.

業 BUSINESS, VOCATION

"His business (業) is building a stand for books out of wood (木)"

ON (ギョウ)	
そつぎょう 卒業: Graduation	こうぎょう 工業: (Manufacturing) industry
じゅぎょう 授業: Lesson	さんぎょう 産業: Industry

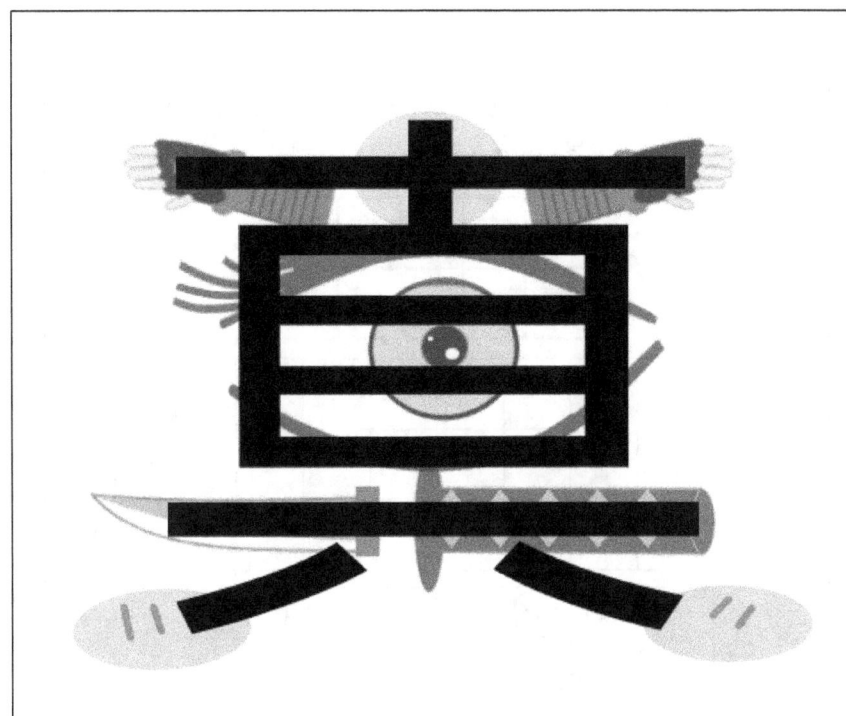

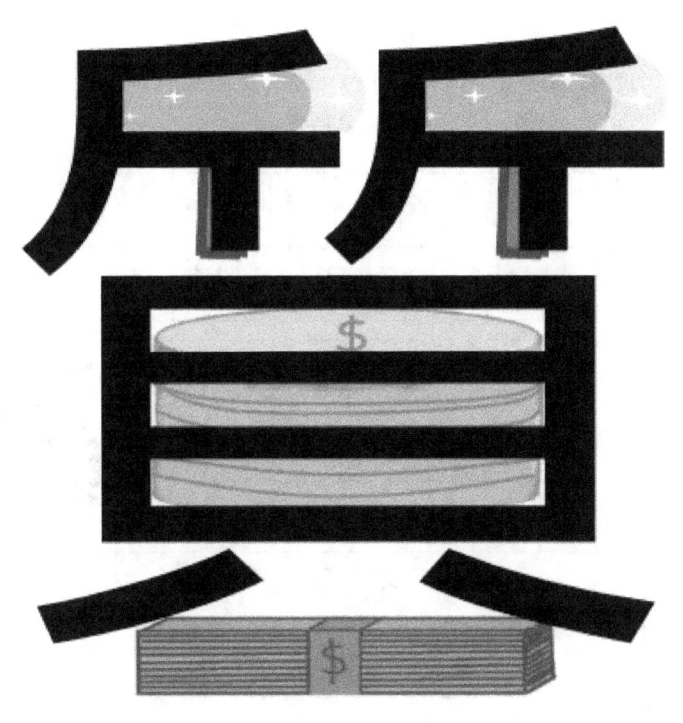

真 TRUE, REALITY

"A true (真) winner is the one who doesn't need ten (十) tools (具), but honest eyes (目)"

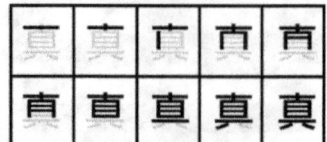

ON (シン)		Kun (ま)		

しゃしん
写真: Photo

ま なか
真ん中: Middle

*This kanji was originally a dead body, considering death as the ultimate truth to be reached.

質 SUBSTANCE, QUALITY

"To buy a good quality (質) axe (斤) you would need a lot of money (貝)"

ON (シツ)

しつもん
質問: Question

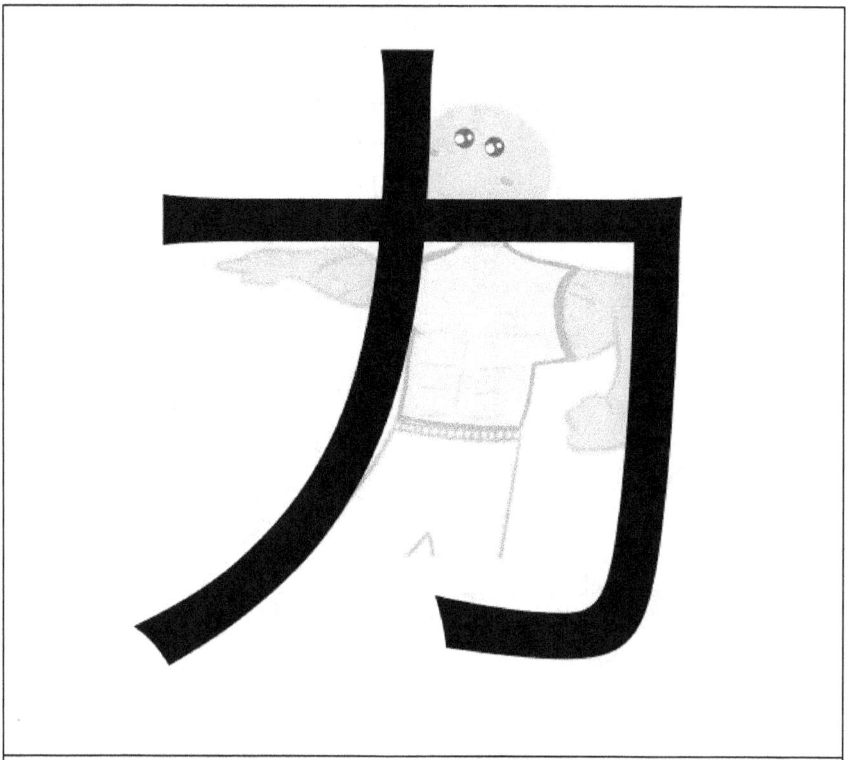

力

病

力 POWER, STRENGTH

"All his strength (力) comes from his muscles"

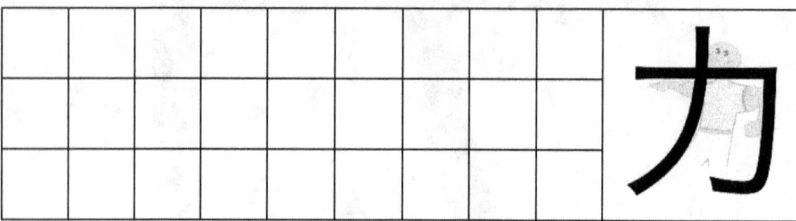

Kun (ちから)
ちから 力 : Force, strength

病 ILL, SICK

"He is always sick (病), but even with his sickness (疒) he ranks third (丙) in his school"

ON (ビョウ)	
びょうき 病気 : Illness	びょういん 病院 : Hospital

特 SPECIAL

"A cow (牛) is a very special (特) animal at the temples (寺) in India"

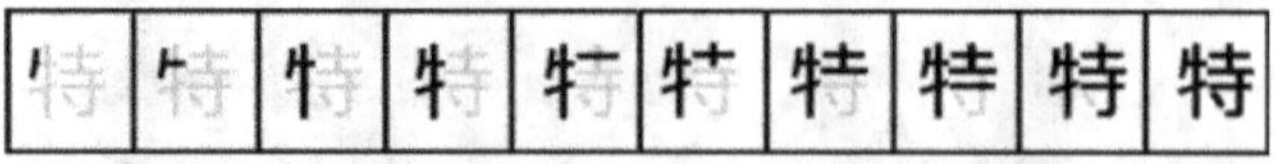

ON (トク)

とっきゅう
特急: Limited express train

とくべつ
特別: Special

とく
特に: Particularly

験 VERIFICAION, TESTING

"The researcher is testing (験) the horse (馬)"

ON (ケン)

しけん
試験: Examination

けいけん
経験: Experience

色 COLOR

"The bent person (⺈) uses dark and light colors (色) for the painting"

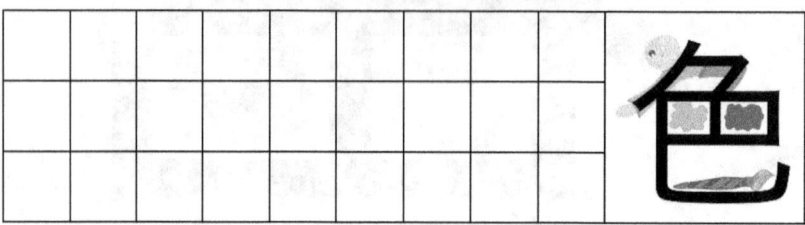

ON (シキ)	Kun (いろ)
けしき 景色: Scene, landscape	いろ 色: Color きいろ 黄色: Yellow ちゃいろ 茶色: Brown

味 FLAVOR, TASTE

"The mouth (口) is not yet (未) ready to taste (味) food coming from the countryside"

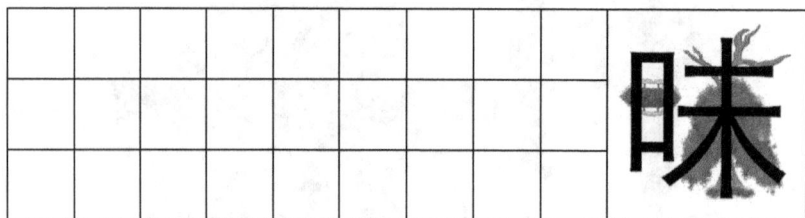

ON (ミ)		Kun (あじ)
きょうみ 興味: An interest しゅみ 趣味: Hobby	いみ 意味: Meaning みそ 味噌: Miso	あじ 味: Taste

料 FEE, MATERIALS

"Both rice (米) and dippers (斗) are materials (料) related to sake"

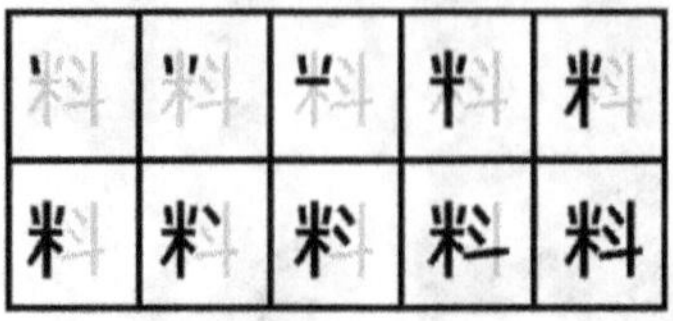

ON (リョウ)	
りょうり 料理: Cooking	しょくりょうひん 食料品: Groceries

旅 TRIP, TRAVEL

"He is admiring the flag pole (㫃) of the of the country he traveled (旅) to"

ON (リョ)	
りょこう 旅行: Travel	りょかん 旅館: Japanese hotel

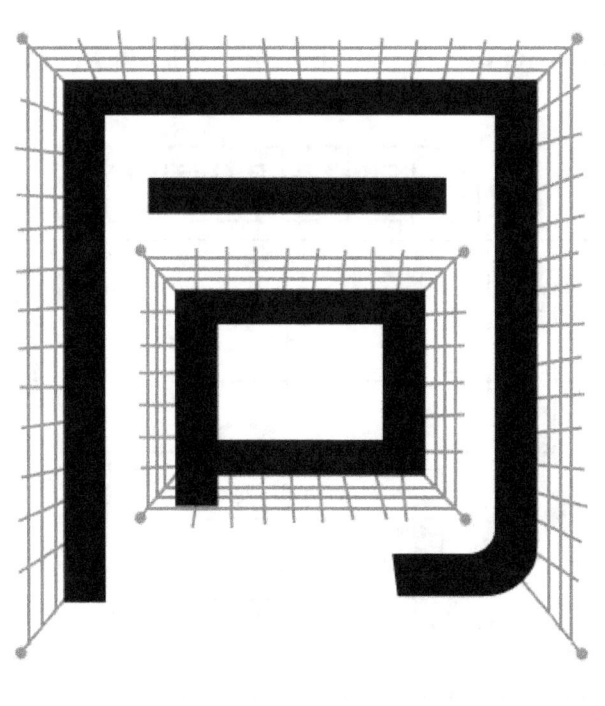

元 BEGINNING, ORIGIN

"At the beginning (元) the man with long legs (儿) wore a hat"

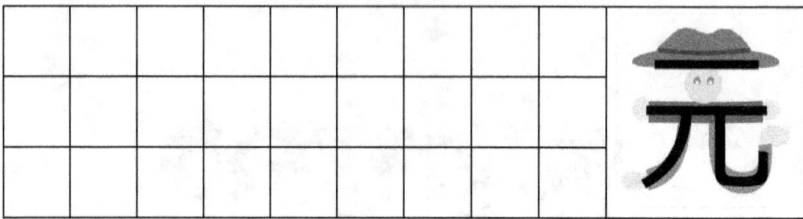

ON (ゲン)	Kun (もと)
げんき 元気：Healthy	もと 元：Origin, source

同 SAME

"The two fences are not the same (同). One has an opening (口) and one does not."

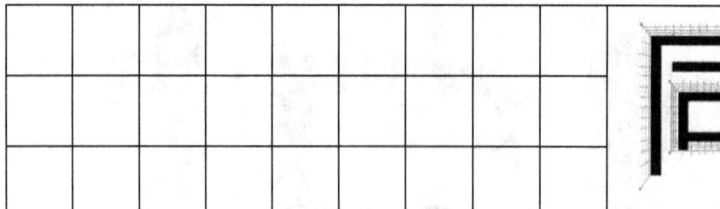

Kun (おな)
おな 同じ：Same

CHAPTER 10: VERBS PART I

仕	売	去	始	回	知
125	126	127	128	129	130
死	切	代	貸	走	起
131	132	133	134	135	136
用	通	考	写	止	歩
137	138	139	140	141	142
		住	注		
		143	144		

仕 ATTEND, SERVE

"The samurai (士) serves (仕) that person (亻)"

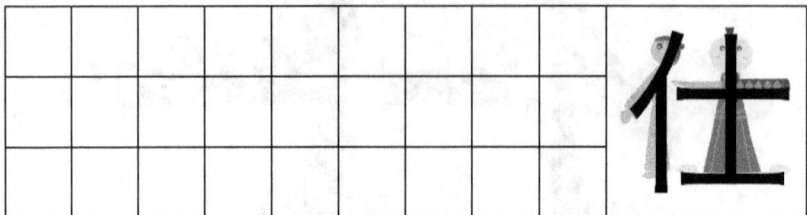

ON (シ)

仕事: Work, job
仕方: Method

売 SELL

"The samurai (士) sells (売) a desk cover (冖) with long wooden legs (儿)"

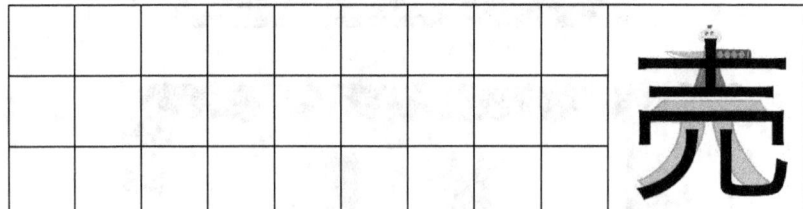

Kun (う)

売る: To sell
売り場: Point of sale

去 GONE, LEAVE

"After I (ム) am gone (去) from this world, only soil (土) will remain"

| 去 | 去 | 去 | 去 | 去 |

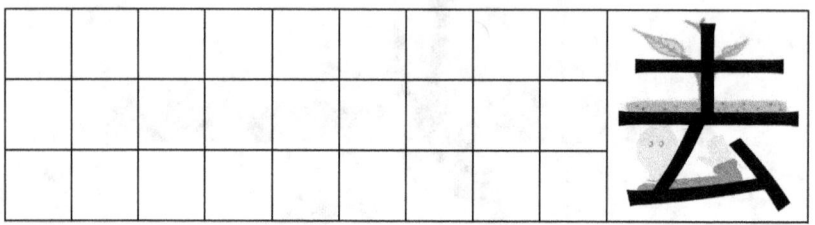

ON (キョ)

去年: Last year

始 COMMENCE, BEGIN

"The act will begin (始) when the woman (女) next to the pedestal (台) says so"

| 始 | 始 | 始 | 始 | 始 | 始 | 始 | 始 |

Kun (はじ)

始まる: (vi) To begin　　始め: Beginning
始める: (vt) To begin

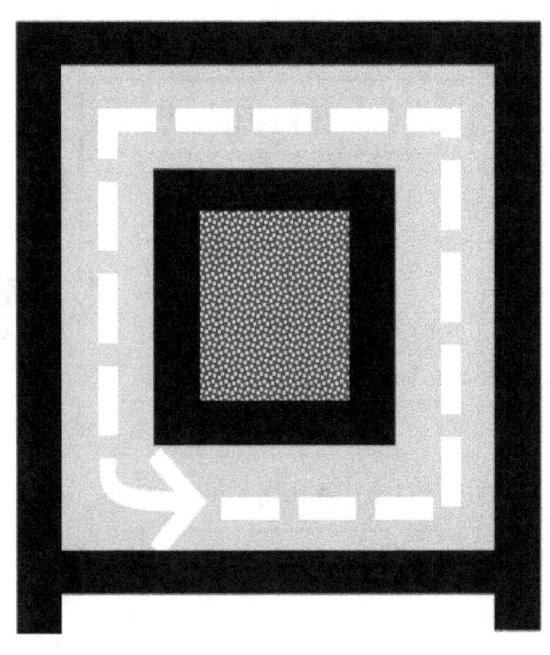

回 TURN, REVOLVE

"The two enclosures (口) allow me to turn (回) around easier"

Kun (まわ)
回る: To turn

知 KNOW, WISDOM

"She knows (知) how to shoot the arrow (矢) so that it would go directly through the opening (口)"

ON (チ)	Kun (し)
承知: Knowledge, awareness	知らせる: To notify 知る: To be aware of, to know

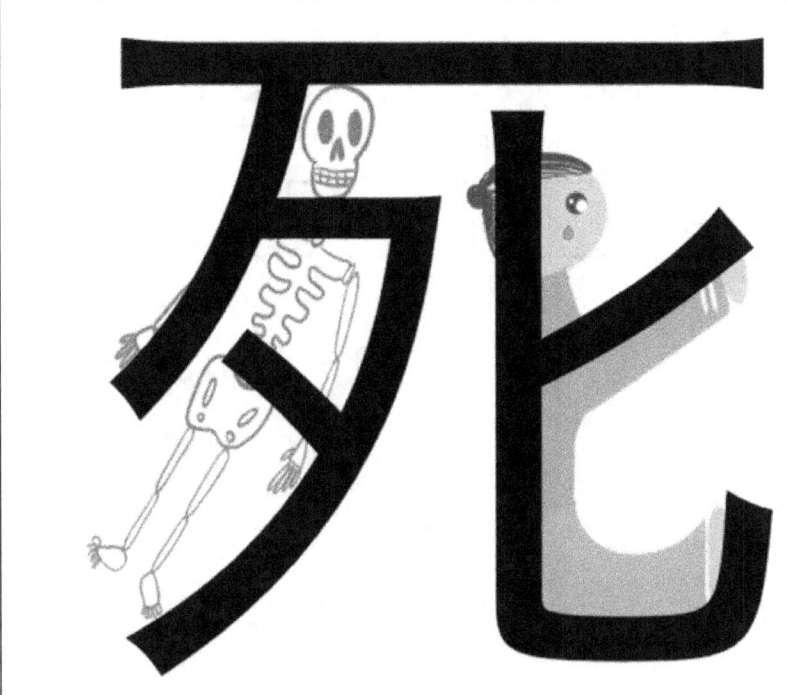

死 DEATH, DIE

"A person mourns the death (歹) of his loved one, while not even knowing why she died (死)"

| 死 | 死 | 死 | 死 | 死 | 死 |

Kun (し)
し 死ぬ: To die

切 CUT, BE SHARP

"Cut (切) the enemy seven (七) times with the sharp sword (刀) and it will bring you victory"

| 切 | 切 | 切 | 切 |

ON (セツ)	Kun (き)
たいせつ 大切: Important しんせつ 親切: Kindness	き 切る: To cut きって 切手: Postage stamp きっぷ 切符: Ticket

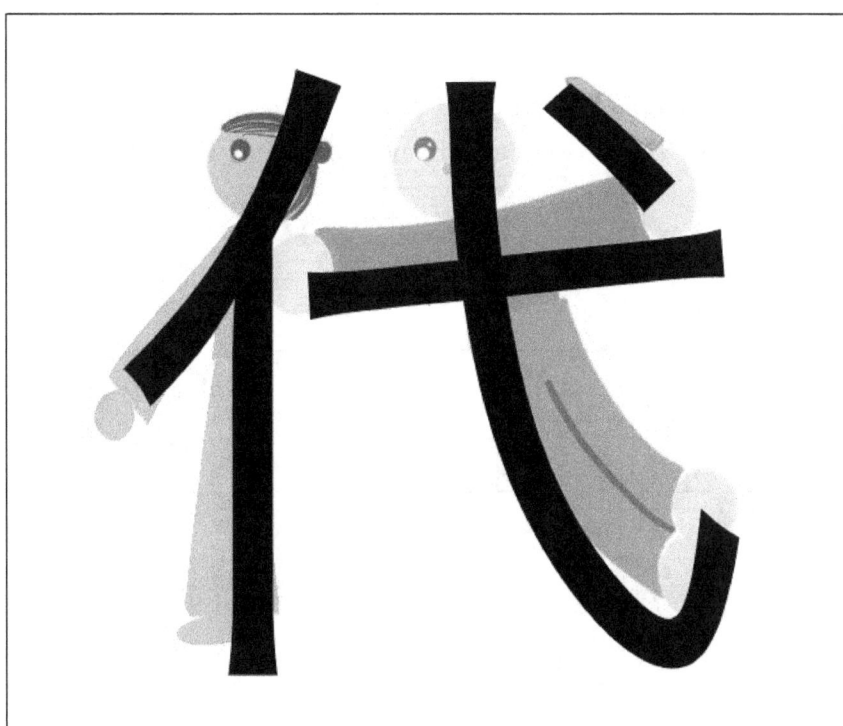

代 SUBSTITUTE, CHANGE

"The person (亻) changes (代) the pointy spikes (弋) that surround the house to avoid having someone getting hurt"

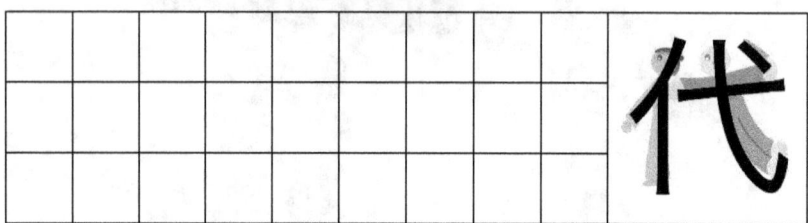

ON (ダイ)	Kun (か)
時代: Era 〜代: 〜Age/period	代わり: Substitute

貸 LEND

"When you lend (貸) money (貝) to someone, the money changes (代) hands, but hopefully, you get it back"

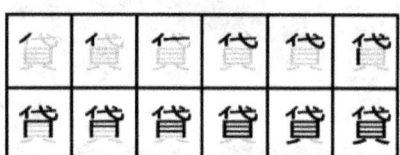

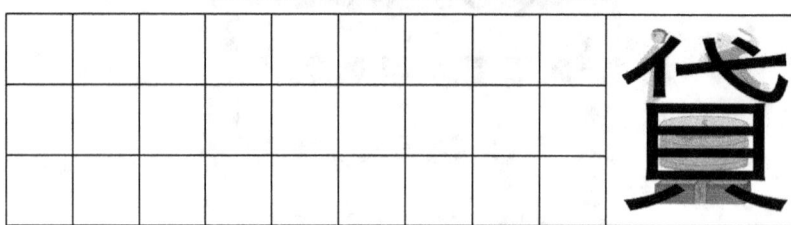

Kun (か)
貸す: To lend

走 RUN

"The boy likes to run (走) on soil (土) without stopping (止)"

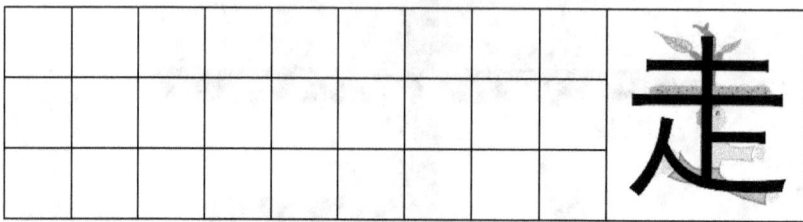

Kun (は し)
はし 走る: To run

起 WAKE UP

"When I wake up (起), I straighten (己) myself up, and then I go for a run (走)"

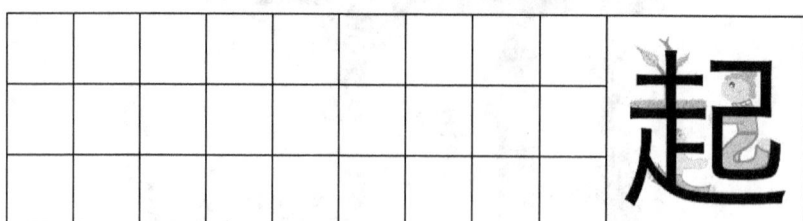

Kun (お, おこ)	
お 起きる: To get up	おこ 起す: To wake someone

用 USE, UTILIZE

"Please use (用) the stairs to go to the second floor"

| 用 | 用 | 用 | 用 | 用 |

ON (ヨウ)	
ようい 用意: Preparation	よう 用: Use
りよう 利用: Utilization	ようじ 用事: Tasks

通 TRAFFIC, COMMUTE

"He uses (用) the stairs by the road (辶) to commute (通) to work"

| 通 | 通 | 通 | 通 | 甬 | 甬 | 甬 | 通 | 通 | 通 |

ON (ツウ)	Kun (とお, かよ)
ふつう 普通: Usually	とお 通る: To go by
こうつう 交通: Traffic, Transportation	かよ 通う: To go to and from

考 CONSIDER, THINK OVER

"The old (耂) lady thinks over (考) her memories"

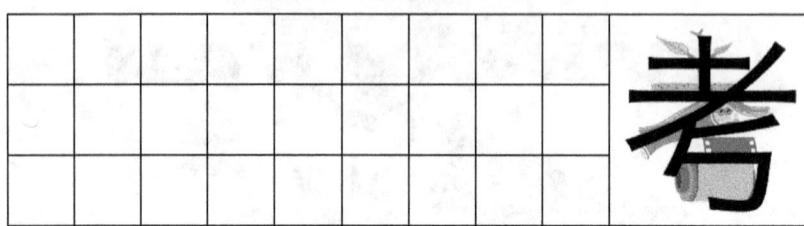

Kun (かんが)
考える: To think about

写 COPY, BE PHOTOGRAPHED

"Models participate (与) in runways to be photographed (写) and win crowns (冖)"

ON (シャ)	Kun (うつ)
写真: Photo	写す: To transcribe, to photograph

*The original meaning of this kanji was "to put things in the house".

止 STOP, HALT

"The policeman stops (止) the girl"

Kun (と, や)	
と 止まる: (vi) To stop (Moving) と 止める: (vt) To stop (Moving)	や 止める: (vt) To stop (an activity) や 止む: (vi) To cease

*The original kanji was the shape of a foot

歩 WALK

"The fewer (少) stops (止) you make, the faster you will walk (歩)"

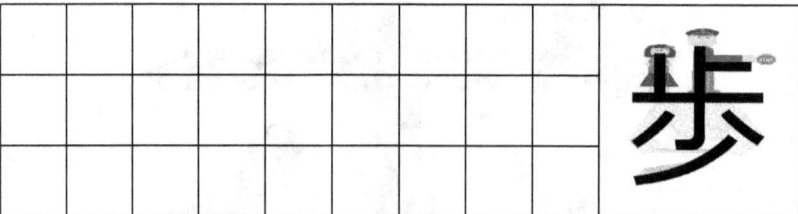

ON (ホ)	Kun (ある)
さんぽ 散歩: Stroll	ある 歩く: To walk

*Originally it was a left foot at the top and a right foot at the bottom.

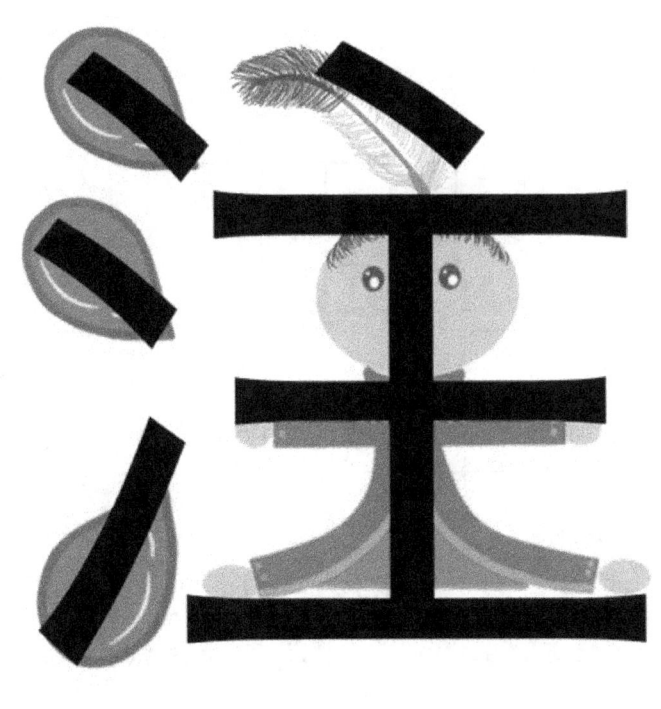

住 DWELL, RESIDE

"The person (亻) protects where his master (主) resides (住)"

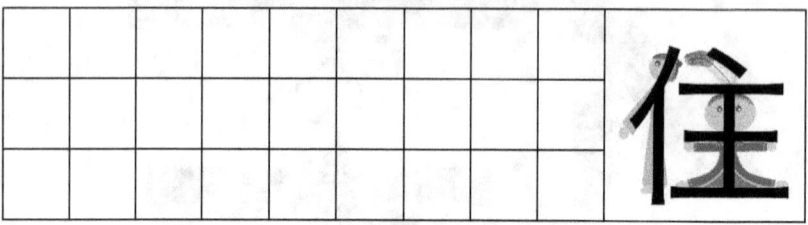

ON (ジュウ)	Kun (す)
住所（じゅうしょ）: An address	住む（す）: To live (of humans)

注 POUR, IRRIGATE

"The chief (主) pours (注) liquid (氵) oil into the lamp to keep the fire burning"

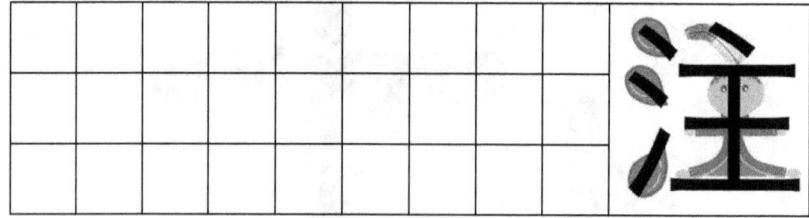

ON (チュウ)	
注意（ちゅうい）: Caution	注射（ちゅうしゃ）: Injection

CHAPTER 11: VERBS PART II

開	研	待	持	急	思
145	146	147	148	149	150
建	帰	作	借	動	働
151	152	153	154	155	156
進	集	合	答	運	転
157	158	159	160	161	162
		勉	別		
		163	164		

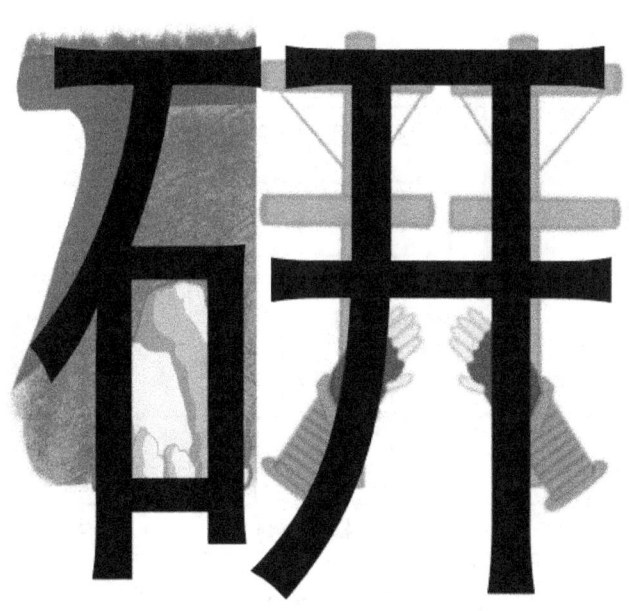

開 OPEN, UNSEAL

"In order to unseal (開) the gate (門) you need to use two poles (开) and two hands"

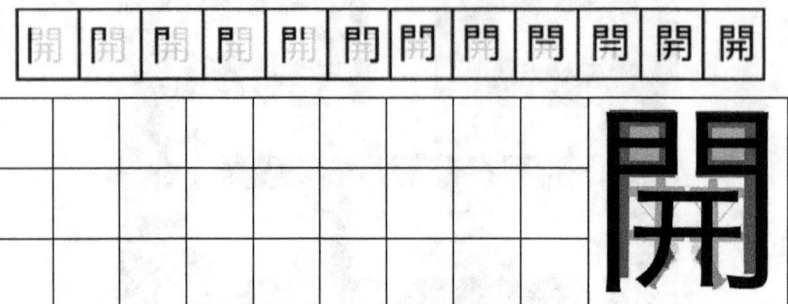

Kun (ひら, あ)
開_あく: (vi) To open (doors), to unwrap
開_{ひら}く: To open (bank account, festival)
開_あける: (vt) To open (a door)

研 POLISH

"Use the two poles (开) to grind to stone (石) and polish (研) it"

ON (ケン)
研究室_{けんきゅうしつ}: Study room, laboratory
研究_{けんきゅう}: Study

待 WAIT

"The traveler will have to wait (待) by the temple (寺) across the road (彳)"

ON (タイ)	Kun (ま)
^{しょうたい} 招待 : Invitation	^ま 待つ: To wait

持 HOLD, HAVE

"Hold (持) your hands (扌) together in the temple (寺)"

Kun (も)	
^も 持つ: To hold	^{き も} 気持ち: Feeling
^{かね も} 金持ち: Rich man	

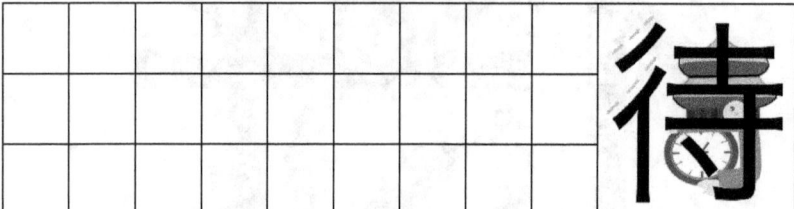
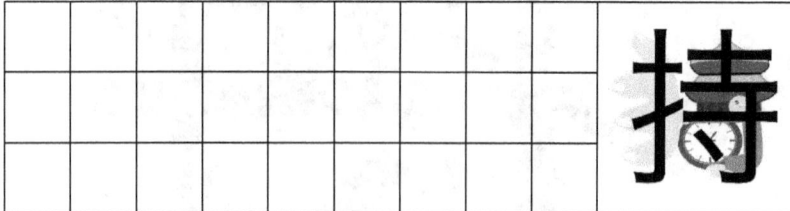

急 HURRY, EMERGENCY

"When the bent person (⺈) hurries (急), his heart (心) beats fast and his hands (ヨ) get swollen"

急 急 急 急 急 急 急 急 急

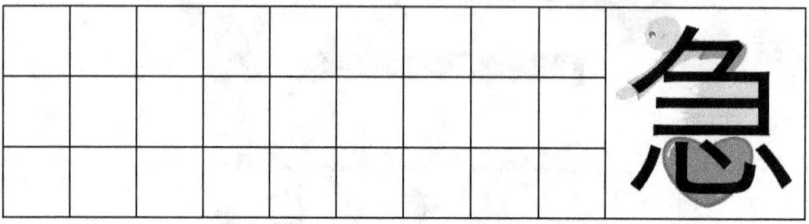

ON (キュウ)	Kun (いそ)
きゅう 急 : Urgent きゅうこう 急 行 : Moving at high speed とっきゅう 特 急 : Limited express train	いそ 急 ぐ : To hurry

思 THINK

"When a person thinks (思), they don't only use their brain (囟) but also their heart (心)"

思 思 思 思 思 思 思 思 思

Kun (おも)	
おも 思 う : To think	おも だ 思 い 出 す : To remember

*Although, very similar to the radical for rice field (田), this kanji actually uses the radical for brain.

建 BUILD

"I'm really stretching (廴) myself trying to build (建) this set of brushes (聿)"

Kun (た、たて)	
建てる: To build	建物: Building
二階建て: Two storied	

帰 HOMECOMING, ARRIVE AT

"Every time I know someone will be arriving at (帰) our house, we use the broom (帚) to clean"

Kun (かえ)	
帰る: To return	帰り: Return

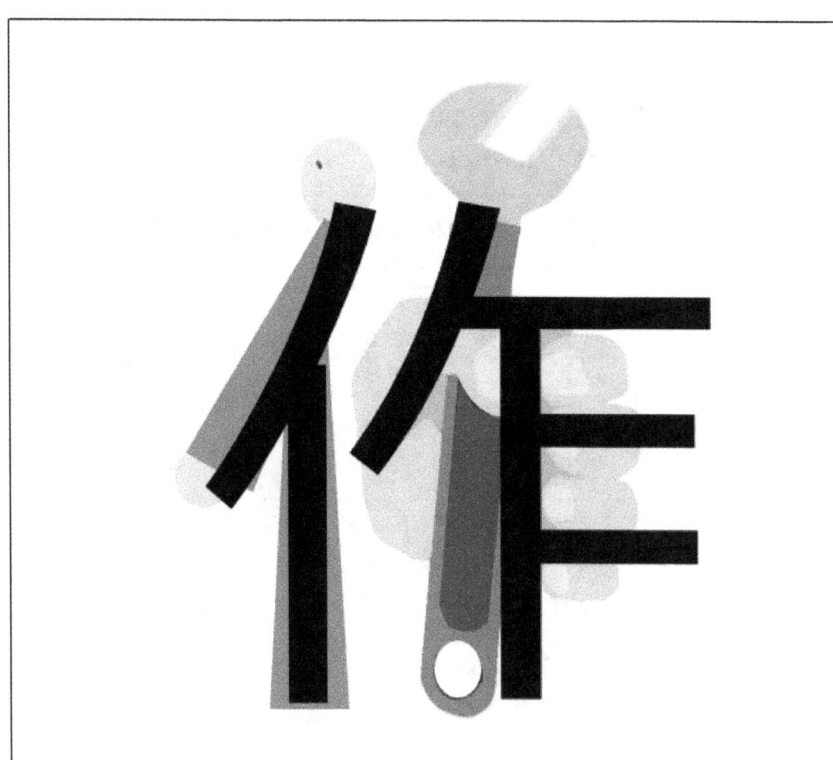

作 MAKE, PRODUCTION

"The person (亻) is getting ready to make (作) something using both, his tools and his hands"

ON (サク)	Kun (つく)
作文(さくぶん): Composition	作る(つく): To make, to produce

借 BORROW

"When a person (亻) borrows (借) too much money, the good life is part of the old days (昔)"

Kun (か)
借りる(か): To borrow

動 MOVE, MOTION

"His strength (力) comes from moving (動) around a lot and lifting heavy (重) weights"

ON (ドウ)		Kun (うご)
どうぶつ 動物: Animal	じどうしゃ 自動車: Automobile	うご 動く: To move
どうぶつえん 動物園: Zoo	うんどう 運動: Exercise	

働 WORK

"When that person (亻) is working (働), he moves (動) around all the time"

Kun (はたら)
はたら 働く: To work

進 ADVANCE, PROGRESS

"The small birds (隹) advance (進) along the road (辶)"

Kun (すす)
進む: To advance

集 GATHER

"All the small birds (隹) gather (集) on that tree (木)"

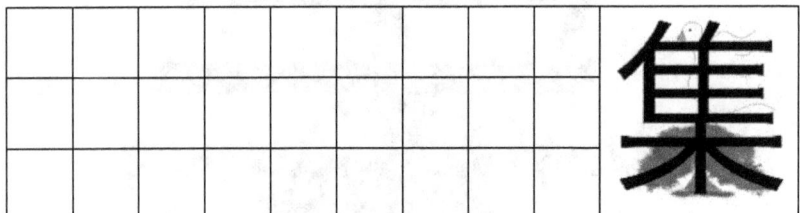

Kun (あつ)
集まる: (vi) To gather
集める: (vt) To collect something

合 FIT, JOIN

"The lid fits (合) well in the opening (口) of that container"

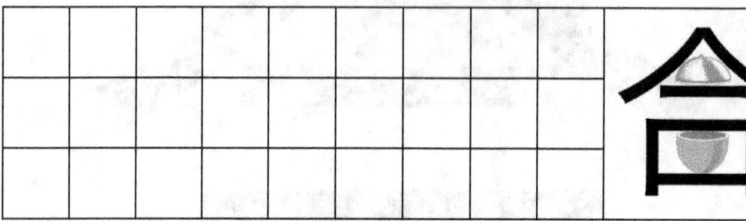

ON (ゴウ)	Kun (あ, あい)	
都合（つごう）: Circumstances	合（あ）う: To come together	試合（しあい）: Game
	具合（ぐあい）: Condition, health	場合（ばあい）: Situation
	間（ま）に合（あ）う: To be in time for	割合（わりあい）: Rate

答 SOLUTION, ANSWER

"The answer (答), that fits (合) our needs, lies inside that container made of bamboo (⺮)"

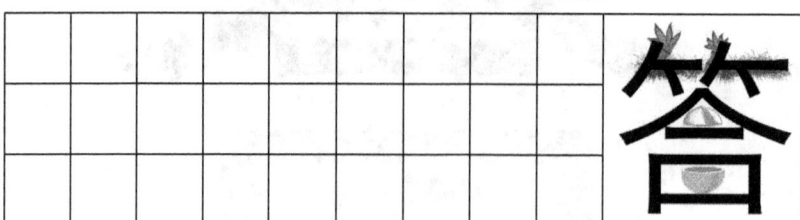

Kun (こた)	
答（こた）える: To answer	答（こた）え: Answer

運 CARRY, TRANSPORT

"The car (車) transports (運) the troops (軍) along the road (辶)"

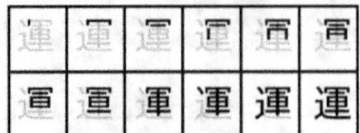

ON (ウン)	Kun (はこ)
うんてんしゅ 運転手: Driver うんてん 運転: Driving	はこ 運ぶ: To carry, to transport

転 TURN AROUND

"He turns around (転) his car (車) so fast, that you only get to see a cloud (云) of smoke behind"

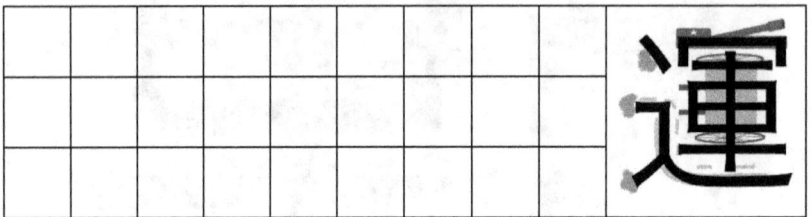

ON (テン)	
じてんしゃ 自転車: Bicycle	うんてんしゅ 運転手: Driver うんてん 運転: Driving

勉 ENCOURAGE, STRIVE

"Don't give me a book full of excuses (免), but instead strive (勉) with all your strength (力)"

ON (ベン)
^{べんきょう}勉強 : Study

別 SEPARATE, DIVERGE

"Knives (刂) are used to separate (別) bones (凸) during dissections"

ON (ベツ)	Kun (わか)
^{とくべつ}特別 : Special ^{べつ}別 : Distinction	^{わか}別れる : To be divided

CHAPTER 12: VERBS PART III

教	好	洗	発	使	映
165	166	167	168	169	170
歌	習	着	有	引	計
171	172	173	174	175	176
究	産	乗	送	終	
177	178	179	180	181	

教 TEACH, DOCTRINE

"The old (耂) lady teaches (教) the child (子) not to hit (攵) others"

ON (キョウ)	Kun (おし)
きょうしつ 教室：Classroom きょうかい 教会：Church きょういく 教育：Education	おし 教える：To teach

好 FOND, LIKE

"The child (子) seems to like (好) that woman (女) very much"

Kun (す)
だいす 大好き：Like very much す 好き：Liking

洗 WASH

"The former (先) soldier washes (洗) his hands and feet with water (氵)"

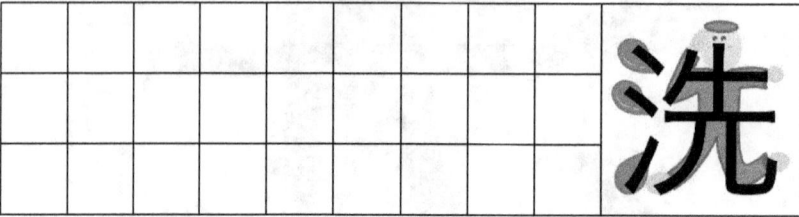

ON (セン)	Kun (あら)
せんたく 洗濯: Laundry	あら 洗う: To wash てあら お手洗い: Toilet

発 DEPARTURE, PUBLISH

"During his departure (発) he was using his legs (儿) to walk with very solid footsteps (癶)"

ON (ハツ)	
はつおん 発音: Pronunciation	しゅっぱつ 出発: Departure

使 USE, ORDER, AMBASSADOR

"The officer (吏) orders (使) the person (イ) to go on a mission"

ON (シ)	Kun (つか)
大使館(たいしかん): Embassy	使う(つか): To use (a thing)

映 REFLECT, PROJECTION

"I'm in the middle (央) of the world seeing a spectacular reflection (映) caused by the sun (日)"

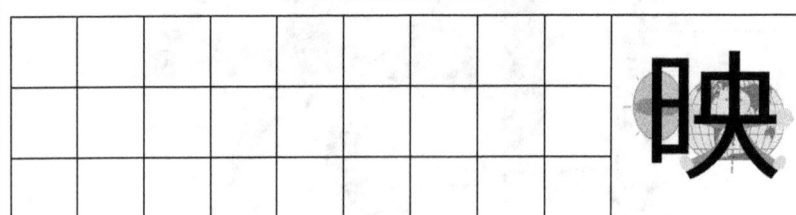

ON (エイ)	
映画(えいが): Movie	映画館(えいがかん): Cinema

歌 SONG, SING

"The two brothers can (可) sing (歌) but they still lack (欠) harmony"

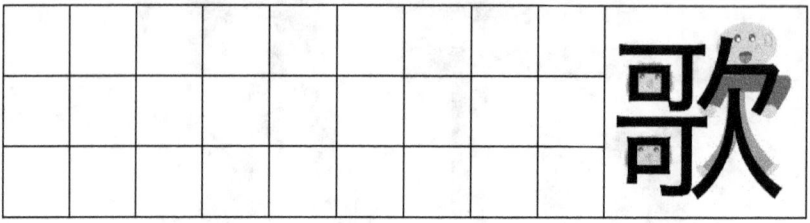

Kun (うた)	
うた 歌: Song	うた 歌う: To sing

習 LEARN

"I learned (習) how to draw an angel with white (白) feathers (羽)"

ON (シュウ)	Kun (なら)
れんしゅう 練習: Practice しゅうかん 習慣: Custom, manners ふくしゅう 復習: Review よしゅう 予習: Preparation for a lesson	なら 習う: To take lessons in

着 ARRIVE, WEAR

"The eye (目) is looking for some sheep's (羊) wool to wear (着)"

Kun (き, ぎ, つ)

着る: To wear	着物: Kimono	上着: Jacket
着く: To arrive at	下着: Underwear	

有 POSSESS, EXIST

"The hand (ナ) posses (有) a piece of meat (月) for survival"

ON (ユウ)

有名: Famous

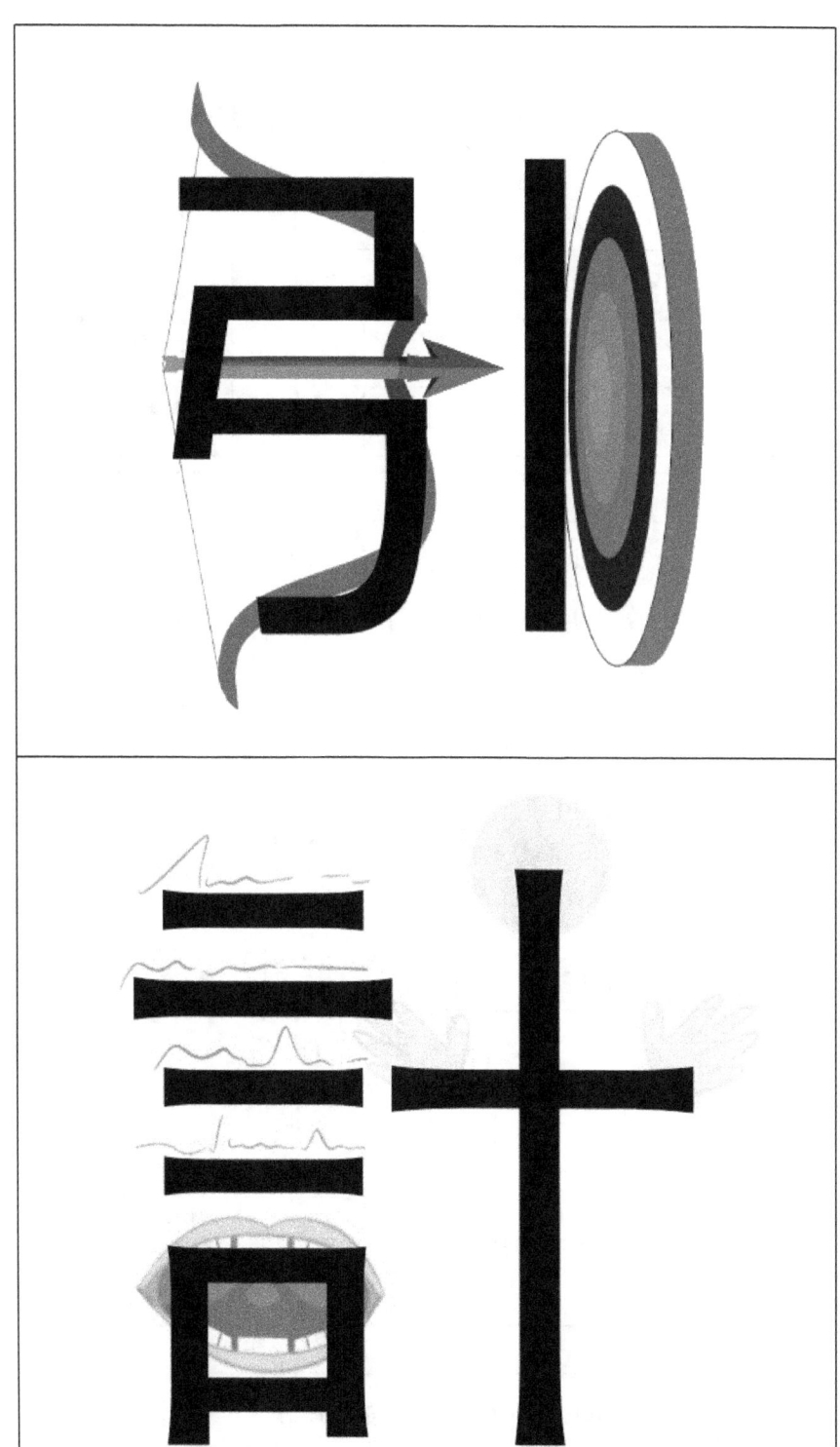

引 PULL

"Pull (引) an arrow through the bow (弓) and hit the mark"

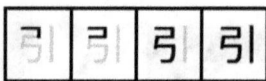

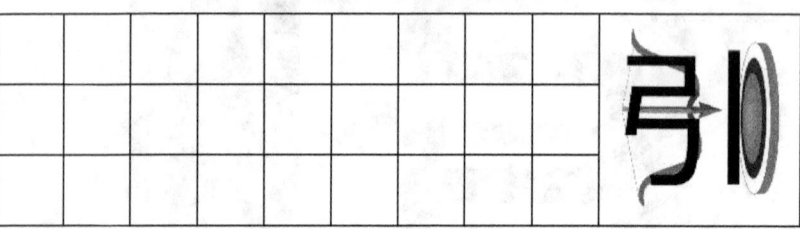

Kun (ひ)

引き出し: Withdrawal

引き出す: To pull out

引っ越す: To move house

引く: To pull

字引: Dictionary

計 PLAN, MEASURE

"During our speech (言), we discussed 10 (十) different ways to measure (計) an object"

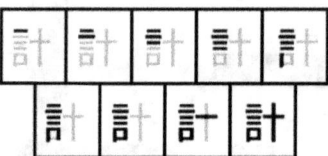

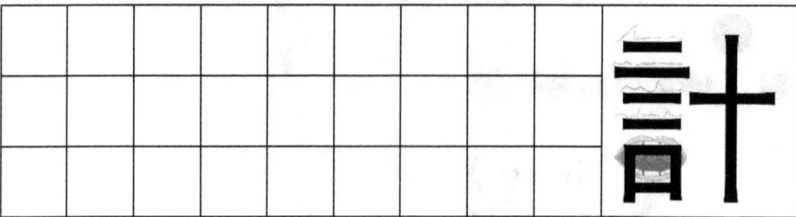

ON (ケイ)

時計: Watch, clock

計画: Plan

究

産

究 RESEARCH, STUDY

"Let's research (究) the nine (九) caves (穴)"

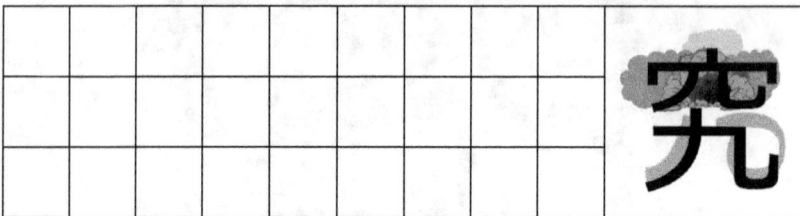

ON (キュウ)

研究 : Study
研究室 : Study room, laboratory

産 PRODUCTS, GIVE BIRTH

"She can't stand (立) up any longer as she is ready to give birth (産) to a new life (生)"

ON (サン)

生産 : Production
産業 : Industry

Reading Exception

お土産 : Souvenir

乗 RIDE, BOARD

"Let's ride (乗) the train!"

Kun (の)
乗り換える: To change (bus, train)
乗る: To get on (train, etc.)
乗り物: Vehicle

*Originally a man on top of a tree. However, the kanji has lost the original shape.

送 SEND

"Please send (送) someone to take the bolt (关) down so that we can use the road (辶)"

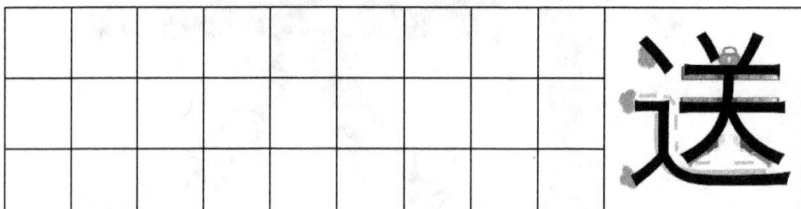

ON (ソウ)	Kun (おく)
放送: Broadcast	送る: To send (a thing)

終 END, FINISH

"This winter (冬) ends (終) and so does my thread (糸)"

Kun (お)
終わる: To finish
終わり: The end

This book covers a 181 Kanji found in the Japanese Language Proficiency Test N4 and the main idea is to cover as much material as possible related to Kanji.

If you wish to join me in this journey of learning Japanese, check out my social media! There you can ask questions and join our conversations!

@JLPTKanjiMnemonics

Also, if you have any suggestions or improvements about my book, feel free to e-mail me at jlptkanjimnemonics@gmail.com

INDEX

～
- ～いん　～員 80
- ～か　～家 90
- ～く　～区 100
- ～だい　～代 170
- ～ちょう　～町 96

あ
- あう　合う 198
- あお　青 112
- あおい　青い 112
- あか　赤 112
- あかい　赤い 112
- あかるい　明るい 110
- あかんぼう　赤ん坊 112
- あき　秋 28
- あく　開く 184
- あける　開ける 184
- あさ　朝 22
- あさごはん　朝ご飯 22, 42
- あじ　味 154
- あした　明日 110
- あす　明日 110
- あたま　頭 56
- あつい　暑い 128
- あつまる　集まる 196
- あつめる　集める 196
- あに　兄 76
- あね　姉 74
- あらう　洗う 208
- あるく　歩く 178
- あんしん　安心 52

い
- いえ　家 90
- いか　以下 138
- いがい　以外 138
- いがく　医学 82
- いけ　池 40
- いけん　意見 144
- いしゃ　医者 82
- いじょう　以上 138
- いそぐ　急ぐ 188
- いちど　一度 140
- いない　以内 138
- いなか　田舎 38
- いぬ　犬 48
- いみ　意味 144, 154
- いもうと　妹 74
- いろ　色 154

う
- うごく　動く 194
- うし　牛 46
- うた　歌 212
- うたう　歌う 212
- うつす　写す 176
- うみ　海 38
- うりば　売り場 86, 162
- うる　売る 162
- うわぎ　上着 214
- うんてん　運転 200
- うんてんしゃ　運転者 200
- うんてんしゅ　運転手 200
- うんどう　運動 194

え
- えいが　映画 64, 210
- えいがかん　映画館 64, 92, 210
- えいご　英語 104
- えんりょ　遠慮 118

お
- おきる　起きる 172
- おくじょう　屋上 88
- おくる　送る 220
- おこす　起す 172
- おしえる　教える 206
- おちゃ　お茶 34
- おてあらい　お手洗い 208
- おと　音 144
- おとうと　弟 76
- おなじ　同じ 158
- おにいさん　お兄さん 76
- おねえさん　お姉さん 74
- おふろ　お風呂 44
- おみやげ　お土産 218
- おもい　重い 116
- おもいだす　思い出す 188
- おもう　思う 188

おや 親 78
およぎかた 泳ぎ方 72
おわり 終わり 222
おわる 終わる 222
おんがく 音楽 144, 146

か

かいがん 海岸 38
かいぎしつ 会議室 88
かいじょう 会場 86
かいもの 買い物 60
かえり 帰り 190
かえる 帰る 190
かお 顔 56
がくもん 学問 136
かじ 火事 60
かす 貸す 170
かぜ 風 44
かぜ 風邪 44
かぞく 家族 72, 90
かた 方 72
かてい 家庭 90
かない 家内 90
かねもち 金持ち 186
かみ 紙 66
かよう 通う 174
かようび 火曜日 24
からだ 体 52
かりる 借りる 192
かるい 軽い 116
かわり 代わり 170
かんがえる 考える 176
かんじ 漢字 104, 134

き

きいろ 黄色 154
きっさてん 喫茶店 34
きって 切手 168
きっぷ 切符 168
きもち 気持ち 186
きもの 着物 214
きゅう 急 188
きゅうこう 急行 188
ぎゅうにく 牛肉 46
ぎゅうにく 牛肉 46
ぎゅうにゅう 牛乳 46
きょういく 教育 206

きょうかい 教会 206
きょうしつ 教室 88, 206
きょうだい 兄弟 76
きょうみ 興味 154
きょねん 去年 164
きる 切る 168
きる 着る 214
ぎんこう 銀行 42
きんじょ 近所 86, 118
きんようび 金曜日 24

く

ぐあい 具合 198
くすり 薬 34
くだもの 果物 60
くび 首 54
くべつ 区別 100
くらい 暗い 110
くろ 黒 114
くろい 黒い 114

け

けいかく 計画 64, 216
けいけん 経験 152
けさ 今朝 22
けしき 景色 154
げつようび 月曜日 24
けん 県 100
げんき 元気 158
けんきゅう 研究 184, 218
けんきゅうしつ 研究室 88, 184, 218
けんぶつ 見物 60

こ

こうぎょう 工業 94, 146
こうじょう 工場 94
こうちゃ 紅茶 34
こうつう 交通 174
こうどう 講堂 94
こうば 工場 94
こうむいん 公務員 80
こえ 声 54
こころ 心 52
ごしゅじん ご主人 78
こたえ 答え 198
こたえる 答える 198
こと 事 60

ことり　小鳥 48
ごはん　ご飯 42
こんど　今度 140
こんや　今夜 20

さ

さいきん　最近 118
さくぶん　作文 134, 192
さむい　寒い 128
さんぎょう　産業 146, 218
さんぽ　散歩 178

し

し　市 98
じ　字 134
しあい　試合 132, 198
しかた　仕方 72, 162
しけん　試験 132, 152
じこ　事故 60
しごと　仕事 60, 162
じしん　地震 40
じだい　時代 170
したぎ　下着 214
したく　支度 140
しつもん　質問 136, 148
じてんしゃ　自転車 70, 200
じどうしゃ　自動車 70, 194
しなもの　品物 62
しぬ　死ぬ 168
じびき　字引 134, 216
じぶん　自分 70
しみん　市民 80, 98
じむしょ　事務所 60, 86
しゃしん　写真 148, 176
じゆう　自由 70
しゅうかん　習慣 212
じゅうしょ　住所 86, 180
じゅぎょう　授業 146
しゅくだい　宿題 136
しゅっぱつ　出発 208
しゅみ　趣味 154
じょうきょう　上京 102
しょうせつ　小説 132
しょうたい　招待 186
しょうち　承知 166
しょくどう　食堂 94
しょくりょうひん　食料品 62, 156

しらせる　知らせる 166
しる　知る 166
しんせつ　親切 78, 168
しんぱい　心配 52

す

すき　好き 206
すすむ　進む 196
すむ　住む 180

せ

せいさん　生産 218
せいよう　西洋 98
せかい　世界 106
せつめい　説明 110, 132
せびろ　背広 126
せわ　世話 106
せんたく　洗濯 208

そ

そつぎょう　卒業 146

た

た　田 38
たいいん　退院 92
だいじ　大事 60
たいしかん　大使館 92, 210
だいすき　大好き 206
たいせつ　大切 168
だいたい　大体 52
だいどころ　台所 62, 86
たいふう　台風 44, 62
ただしい　正しい 122
たてもの　建物 60, 190
たてる　建てる 190
たのしい　楽しい 146
たのしみ　楽しみ 146
たのしむ　楽しむ 146
たべもの　食べ物 60

ち

ちかい　近い 118
ちかく　近く 118
ちかてつ　地下鉄 40
ちから　力 150
ちく　地区 100
ちず　地図 40, 64

ちゃいろ 茶色 34, 154
ちゅうい 注意 144, 180
ちゅうしゃ 注射 180
ちり 地理 40, 140

つ

つかう 使う 210
つく 着く 214
つくる 作る 192
つごう 都合 102, 198
つよい 強い 120

て

てがみ 手紙 66
てんいん 店員 80

と

と 都 102
とうきょう 東京 102
どうぶつ 動物 60, 194
どうぶつえん 動物園 194
とおい 遠い 118
とおく 遠く 118
とおる 通る 174
とくに 特に 152
とくべつ 特別 152, 202
とけい 時計 216
ところ 所 86
としょかん 図書館 64, 92
とっきゅう 特急 152, 188
とまる 止まる 178
とめる 止める 178
どようび 土曜日 24
とり 鳥 48
とりにく とり肉 46

な

なつ 夏 26
なつやすみ 夏休み 26
ならう 習う 212

に

にかいだて 二階建て 190
にく 肉 46
にちようび 日曜日 24
にもつ 荷物 60
にゅういん 入院 92

にゅうじょう 入場 86

の

の 野 36
のみもの 飲み物 60
のりかえる 乗り換える 220
のりもの 乗り物 220
のる 乗る 220

は

ばあい 場合 86, 198
はいしゃ 歯医者 82
はこぶ 運ぶ 200
はじまる 始まる 164
はじめ 始め 164
はじめる 始める 164
ばしょ 場所 86
はしる 走る 172
はたらく 働く 194
はつおん 発音 144, 208
はやい 早い 22
はやし 林 32
はる 春 28
ばんごはん 晩ご飯 42

ひ

ひかり 光 44
ひかる 光る 44
ひきだし 引き出し 216
ひきだす 引き出す 216
ひく 引く 216
ひくい 低い 124
ひこうじょう 飛行場 86
びじゅつかん 美術館 92
ひっこす 引っ越す 216
びょういん 病院 92, 150
びょうき 病気 150
ひらく 開く 184
ひる 昼 24
ひるごはん 昼ご飯 24, 42
ひるま 昼間 24
ひるやすみ 昼休み 24
ひろい 広い 126

ふ

ふく 服 66
ふくしゅう 復習 212

ぶたにく　豚肉 46
ふつう　普通 174
ふとい　太い 126
ふとる　太る 126
ふべん　不便 114, 138
ふゆ　冬 26
ぶんか　文化 134
ぶんがく　文学 134
ぶんしょう　文章 134
ぶんぽう　文法 134

へ

べつ　別 202
へや　部屋 88
べんきょう　勉強 120, 202
へんじ　返事 60
べんり　便利 114

ほ

ほうそう　放送 220

ま

まいあさ　毎朝 22
まち　町 96
まつ　待つ 186
まにあう　間に合う 198
まわる　回る 166
まんが　漫画 64
まんなか　真ん中 148

み

みじかい　短い 124
みそ　味噌 154

む

むら　村 96
むり　無理 140

も

もういちど　もう一度 140
もくようび　木曜日 24
もつ　持つ 186
もと　元 158
もの　者 82
もの　物 60

もり　森 32
もん　門 90
もんだい　問題 136

や

やおや　八百屋 88
やさい　野菜 36
やむ　止む 178
やめる　止める 178

ゆ

ゆうがた　夕方 20, 72
ゆうはん　夕飯 20, 42
ゆうびんきょく　郵便局 114
ゆうべ　昨夜 20
ゆうめい　有名 214

よ

よう　用 174
ようい　用意 144, 174
ようじ　用事 60, 174
ようふく　洋服 66, 98
よしゅう　予習 212
よる　夜 20
よわい　弱い 120

り

りゆう　理由 140
りよう　利用 174
りょうしん　両親 78
りょうほう　両方 72
りょうり　料理 140, 156
りょかん　旅館 92, 156
りょこう　旅行 156

れ

れんしゅう　練習 212

わ

わかれる　別れる 202
わたくし　私 70
わたし　私 70
わりあい　割合 198
わるい　悪い 122

www.ingramcontent.com/pod-product-compliance
Lightning Source LLC
Chambersburg PA
CBHW051428290426
44109CB00016B/1474